FOR BETTER, FOR WORSE

For Better, For Worse

Devotional Thoughts for Married Couples

DEVOTIONAL THOUGHTS FOR MARRIED COUPLES

COMPILED AND EDITED BY

MARLENE BAGNULL

CHRISTIAN PUBLICATIONS, INC.
CAMP HILL, PENNSYLVANIA

CHRISTIAN PUBLICATIONS, INC.

3825 Hartzdale Drive, Camp Hill, PA 17011
www.christianpublications.com

Faithful, biblical publishing since 1883

For Better, For Worse
ISBN: 0-88965-214-7
LOC Catalog Card Number: 2003-110704

© 2003 by Marlene Bagnull

*Note: Italicized words in Scripture quotations
are the emphasis of the author.*

The Unfolding of a Rose
Marlene Bagnull

Our relationship is like a beautiful rosebud

    beginning to unfold.

It needs nurture, water, sunlight,

    cultivation and pruning.

We nurture our relationship

    through talking and listening.

We water it through our laughter and tears.

We give it sunlight

    through letting our love shine brightly,

    telling and showing our spouse how special he is.

We cultivate it

    through our thoughtfulness.

We prune it through making the decision to love

    in the midst of difficulties, hurts and disagreements.

And the One who created the rose—

the One who daily cultivates the garden of our hearts—

    will be with us always,

    shining the light of His love upon us.

Contents

Part Two: For Better or Worse

Part Three: For Richer, for Poorer

Part Four: In Sickness and Health

Part Five: Forsaking All Others

Part Six: To Love and to Cherish

Part Seven: Till Death Do Us Part

Acknowledgments

With deep appreciation to my husband, Paul,
and to the husbands and wives
who made this book possible
by living the vows they made
on their wedding days
and by sharing their stories.

From Me to You

Marlene Bagnull, compiler and editor

"Reading your book made me fall more deeply in love with my husband!"

It was the highest compliment I could pay a friend who had asked me to review her in-progress-but-not-yet-published novel. And I meant what I said! The twists and turns of her storyline caused me to care about her characters so much that I actually found myself praying for them—that is, until I remembered they were only make-believe! Still, their story had a profound impact on my life and caused me to love and appreciate my husband, Paul, much more than I could have imagined on November 9, 1963, when we said, "I do."

I'm praying the stories in this book will have a similar impact on you, for they are *true* stories about real people—people who are choosing to live out the vows they made on their wedding days. Their choices, same as ours, aren't always easy. The temptation to put our own spin on the promises we made is always present.

To have and to hold . . . and to control.

For better or worse . . . as long as there's more better than worse.

For richer or poorer . . . but love doesn't pay the bills!

In sickness and health . . . but I didn't sign on to be a doctor or nurse.

Forsaking all others . . . but can't I at least look?

To love and to cherish . . . when that's how my mate treats me!

Till death do us part . . . You mean there's no escape clause?

Today some couples do write their own vows, but the key word, *commitment,* may not be included or taken seriously. After all, we live in a free country and we have a "right" to be happy. But marriage is about so much more than "living happily ever after." Some of the most special memories Paul and I share are not of "happy" times but of tough times when it was only our love for each other—and God's love for us—that enabled us to go through and grow through problems we would have preferred to avoid. Our marriage is stronger because we've chosen to live out the commitment we made on our wedding day and to face—together—the "challenges and opportunities" (as a friend encouraged us to view them) that are a part of life.

God promises that "nothing . . . is ever wasted" (1 Corinthians 15:58, TLB) and that "all that happens to us is working for our good if we love God and are fitting into his plans" (Romans 8:28, TLB). And remember, God "speaks no careless word" (Psalm 12:6, TLB)!

But God's plan is more than for married couples to simply endure "till death do us part." He longs for each husband and wife to know the joy of being cherished by their mate—not just some days, but *every* day.

Even though we've been married for thirty-eight years, twice this week Paul brought me flowers just to say, "I love you." Last night he took me to a contemporary worship service even though he was tired and it's not the style of worship he prefers. "I know you need to go to church tonight, honey," he said. And he was right! Someone I care about had hurt me deeply and I was really, really down! Paul did what he always does. He listened. He put his arms around me. And he reminded me in word and deed that I am cherished.

Some of you may be just beginning your journey together as husband and wife. May you feel the authors of this book cheering you on to work at your marriage so that the love you feel today becomes stronger and deeper with each passing year. For those who have been married a long time, may these stories touch your hearts and cause you to fall even more deeply in love with your spouses. And may we all be encouraged to strengthen our commitments to one another and to the Lord so that He may be able to point to us and say, "See how they love one another!"

Advice to a Groom

Bob Hostetler

The Bible says, "He who finds a wife finds what is good and receives favor from the LORD" (Proverbs 18:22) and "Houses and wealth are inherited from parents, but a prudent wife is from the LORD" (19:14).

Your bride is God's gift to you. "She is worth far more than rubies" (31:10) or any other treasure. Always treat her like God's gift. Never allow any earthly thing—not a job, not a ministry, not a football game, not another friendship—to take priority over her.

As unlikely as it may seem today, you will have disagreements. Some of them might be loud. But the Song of Solomon refers to the "little foxes" that ruin the vineyards (Song of Solomon 2:15). I urge you not to ignore even the smallest disagreements, because left alone, they can wreak havoc on a marriage. Keep short accounts with your bride. Never walk away while she is crying; never lay a hand on her except in love; and "Do not let the sun go down while you are still angry" (Ephesians 4:26).

It would probably be best if you don't try to get inside her head; you'll just get lost in all the twists and turns in there (it's not like a man's head). Instead, concentrate on getting into her heart; try to *feel* what she's feeling when she's feeling it, and you'll probably end up understanding her much better. Simply observe what pleases her and what irritates her and work tirelessly to increase the former and decrease the latter.

The Bible also instructs you to "rejoice in the wife of your youth" (Proverbs 5:18). Revel in her. Bask in her smile. Delight in her laughter. Spend time with her. Pray with her. Soak up her words. Keep dating her after the wedding. Kiss her often . . . and long. Say "I love you" every day of your life. Try never to miss an opportunity to tell her she's beautiful. Do whatever it takes to remember her birthday and your anniversary. Save as much money as you can, but never cut corners on gifts . . . or lingerie! Ask her for forgiveness when you need it, and ask her for advice even when you don't need it.

I charge you also with words from the book of Malachi: "Guard yourself in your spirit, and do not break faith with the wife of your youth" (Malachi 2:15). Build hedges around your marriage. Set boundaries that will guard your heart and preserve your integrity and ensure that you never break faith with the wife of your youth.

And finally, remember that the biblical model for a husband is a man who willingly died for His Bride. So I charge you to do as the Bible says and love your wife "just as Christ loved the church and gave himself up for her" (Ephesians 5:25). Love her. Give yourself up for her. Lay down your life—day after day—for her. Strive always to be the man she deserves, and you'll be amazed at how she remains exactly what you desire.

Advice to a Bride

Bob Hostetler

Your wedding day is a precious gift from God, a day when family and friends surround you and bless you, expressing their love and joy and support for you and your groom. But if you could possibly take all their smiling faces and put them together, they still wouldn't be as big as the smile your heavenly Father wears as He looks down on you on your special day. "As a bridegroom rejoices over his bride, so . . . your God [is rejoicing] over you" (Isaiah 62:5) right now.

Still, as wonderful and beautiful as your wedding is, it's only one day . . . and a wedding does not make a marriage. If you are going to be what Scripture calls a "wife of noble character" (Proverbs 31:10), it's going to take a daily commitment—a daily decision to renew your vows to your groom.

Remember that marriages—even those made in heaven—are not perfect, and neither is the groom! There will be times when your husband will perplex, anger and irritate you. There will be days when dirty socks on the floor, lack of communication and puzzling priorities make you want to put him out on Tuesday with the trash. But those are the times when a "wife of noble character" will prove herself. Those are the times when, if you would be fully loved, you must love him fully, because it is when your love is challenged the most that it will shine the brightest.

Speaking of that, I urge you not to shoot for perfection in your marriage; instead, shoot for intimacy. And the only way to be intimate with another person is to be vulnerable about who you are, what you think and what you feel. Let it always be the real you that your husband is in love with and not some variation or imitation.

Also, keep in mind that marriage is not a duet; it is a trio. Therefore, show yourself to be a woman of God in everything you do. After all, this is one of the reasons your groom chose you in the first place, and you can do nothing better to strengthen and preserve your marriage than to remember that "charm is deceptive, and beauty is fleeting; but a woman who fears the LORD is to be praised" (Proverbs 31:30).

Seek out older women to mentor you, as the Bible commands in Titus 2:3-5. Look for godly women who have solid marriages and learn from them.

I advise you to make your mother-in-law your best friend. No woman on earth knows your groom any better than she does, and that's wisdom that can't be bought for any amount of money.

And be sensitive to your parents too, as they adjust—not so much to your groom, but to their daughter as a *wife*! The Bible is clear that you and your new husband must truly and completely leave your parents and cleave to each other, but that won't always be an easy process for your mom and dad. Help them through it, even as you make sure that your groom is always your top priority.

And finally, don't ever ask yourself, "How can I get more out of my marriage?" or even, "How can my husband get more out of our marriage?" Ask, "How can God get more glory from our marriage?" With that kind of attitude, the things of earth will grow strangely dim in the light of the glory God bestows on your marriage. And your husband will arise and call you blessed, saying, "Many women do noble things, but you surpass them all" (Proverbs 31:29).

PART ONE

To Have and to Hold

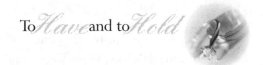

Happily Ever After?

Diana L. James

For I know the plans I have for you, says the Lord. They are plans for good and not for evil, to give you a future and a hope. (Jeremiah 29:11, TLB)

The wedding was beautiful. Flowers, harpists, fabulous food, family, friends, my dress—all of it picture-perfect. Almost like a dream.

Now it was the first morning of our honeymoon at a lovely resort hotel on the California coast. I awakened at dawn to the chirping of birds in the pine trees outside our window. Through the pines I caught glimpses of white breakers gently splashing on dark rocks along the shore.

Max lay next to me, sleeping peacefully. Yesterday he had looked like Prince Charming in his pearl-grey tuxedo, bow tie, boutonniere and cummerbund. But this morning, as I looked over at him, I felt a sudden clutch of fear.

My thoughts swirled crazily. *Who is this man? What have I done? Oh God, did I make a mistake?*

A nagging inner voice harassed me. *We're so different. This is never going to work. He's a perfectionist, and I'm just a "take-it-easy, happy-go-lucky, don't worry about things" kind of person. We'll drive each other crazy.*

I bowed my head. *Oh Lord, help me. I'm so afraid this marriage can't possibly work.*

Max stirred. He rolled over, opened one sleepy eye, sat up and smiled at me. His hair, so perfectly combed for our wedding yesterday, now stood up all over the top of his head and formed a long, high, Kewpie-doll kind of curl.

In spite of my best efforts, I just couldn't hold back a snicker. Max glanced over at the mirror and let out a loud guffaw.

Pretending to pout, I said, "Someone took away my handsome Prince Charming and left me a Kewpie doll."

We both got the giggles then and laughed until we cried. A wave of relief swept over me. I felt a new sense of confidence and trust. God had answered my small prayer and swept away my big fear. He helped me see that, with humor, Max and I could overcome our differences and make our marriage work.

Through the years, whenever our different personalities have clashed, we've found that same formula solves almost everything: Pray first—then find some bit of shared humor to reduce fear, defuse anger and melt disagreements. It works for us. I can almost guarantee it will work for you too.

Lord, thank You for the gifts of humor and prayer, and thank You for showing us how to make this marriage work—despite our differences. Amen.

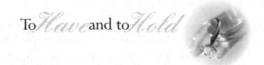

Double Wedding Ring

Lucinda Secrest McDowell

They will be my people, and I will be their God. I will give them sin-
gleness of heart and action, so that they will always fear me for their
own good and the good of their children after them. I will make an ev-
erlasting covenant with them: I will never stop doing good to them.
(Jeremiah 32:38-40)

As I glance at the Double Wedding Ring quilt on our bed, I ponder the significance of those two forever-intertwining circles and
how fragile they can be in real life.

My husband once removed his wedding ring in the middle of a
disagreement and put it on the table beside me. I was crushed.
He had every right to be frustrated, even angry. But even though
I could sympathize with Mike's exasperation at the time, I still
felt that taking off his ring was going a bit too far.

In a few minutes Mike also thought better of his actions, and
his wedding ring went back on. (Whew!)

Even in the heat of the moment, we both remembered the
part of our double-wedding-ring ceremony where the minister
emphasized that the circular ring is a symbol of eternal love without end. "With this ring, I thee wed. . . ."

I doubt any bride or groom on his or her wedding day ever
dreams of a time when he or she might be sorely tempted to remove
that symbol of lasting love. But sometimes the feelings of love don't

last. And it is in these times that a symbol, like a wedding ring, serves as a reminder of our covenant with one another and with God.

I'll be the first to admit that when I finally entered the blissful state of matrimony at age thirty-one, I brought with me some pretty unrealistic expectations. Of course, you couldn't have convinced me of that at the time.

I realize now that I viewed marriage as a sort of "selective service," or as living in a dependent/independent relationship. In other words, when I wanted to be independent, I would be. And when I wanted to be dependent on Mike, then, by golly, he'd better be dependable!

But we can't selectively decide in marriage what days to show mutual love, obedience, respect and servanthood any more than we can in a life of following Christ. The world says, "If it feels good, do it. And when it doesn't feel good any more, leave." God says, "I have made a covenant with you, and you have made a covenant with one another. I will give you what you need to keep that covenant." And our wedding rings stand as a symbol of that promise to one another before God.

Just as my Double Wedding Ring quilt comforts me during cold New England winters, my wedding ring is a comfort and reminder not only of Mike's love, but of God's covenant with us.

Dear heavenly Father, I confess that there are times when I don't feel like loving, but when I am reminded of Your faithfulness to me, it helps me daily fulfill my own covenant of love to my husband. Thank You for Your love without end and for the tangible reminder of our wedding rings. Amen!

[Adapted from *Quilts From Heaven—Finding Parables in the Patchwork of Life,* © 1999 Lucinda Secrest McDowell. Published by Broadman & Holman Publishers.]

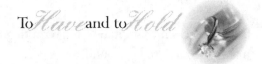

From This Day Forth

Jana Carman

Be kind . . . forgiving each other, just as in Christ God forgave you.
(Ephesians 4:32)

Over the years, we have had several beagles. Hounds like to find the carcass of a dead animal (the riper the better) and roll in it.

I hate to admit it, but sometimes I get a similar perverted pleasure from reliving details of how so-and-so mistreated me. When the "so-and-so" is my husband, this grubbing in the garbage of resentment proves unhealthy for me and for my marriage.

Scarcely was the honeymoon over before I found I had married a flawed human being—just like myself. John had some habits that irritated me. (I had one or two that exasperated him as well.) Although we had been engaged for eighteen months, we discovered there were many nice and not-so-nice surprises as we began to work at melding our lives together.

Misunderstandings, unspoken expectations, the tension of differing family backgrounds—it is a wonder that any marriage survives. Our love helps, but patience, forgiveness and refusing to hold a grudge undergird the love.

The wedding promise, "to have and to hold, from this day forth," looks in only one direction. In building a marriage, every day needs to be "from this day forth." Burying yesterday's "garbage" reduces my temptation to go rooting through it. And that makes me nicer to be around!

Thank You, Lord, that You put my trespasses out of mind and no longer hold them against me. Help me to be like You. Amen.

Committed

Learning to know you, and be known,
means going, layer after layer,
deeper and deeper
beneath the skin that others know,
into the strength and sweetness
at the heart.

Sometimes—
as in peeling onions—
we cry so hard we can't see what we're doing.
But I don't give up onions for that reason
Nor will I give up you.

—*Jana Carman*

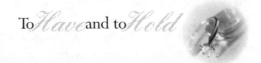

Unconditional Commitment

Nancy Stoppelkamp

May the God who gives endurance and encouragement give you a spirit of unity among yourselves as you follow Christ Jesus, so that with one heart and mouth you may glorify the God and Father of our Lord Jesus Christ. Accept one another, then, just as Christ accepted you, in order to bring praise to God. (Romans 15:5-7)

Sheltered by huge umbrellas, I felt like a queen walking from the church to our home reception, determined not to allow a little rain to spoil our wedding day. Our reception was a loving send-off, with guitars and singing. We both loved music. Our opposite backgrounds and few differences certainly wouldn't matter. . . .

I soon discovered that the very things that attracted us to each other also carried challenging dimensions. I admired Fred's intelligence, but he lived in his thoughts, convinced he knew everything. He was touched by my sensitive spirit, but I often lived in my emotions. I had always wanted a husband with drive and motivation, but soon his drive drove me up the wall. My flexibility was admirable, but not my disorganization. Our pastor said we were more opposite than any couple he'd ever known, but we gradually learned to meet in the middle.

Our commitment to each other helped when I was alone with three children under five. Besides his regular job, Fred attended seminary, Junior Jaycees and the ski patrol at night. He also restored cars at home. He was very gifted—but not with changing diapers and being with little ones. His commitment to me sustained him when I was chronically ill.

Fred loved hiking with our maturing children, and we camped every other weekend. I enjoyed it more once our babies outgrew diapers. Fred ignored spiders in the tent and strange sounds outside and slept soundly in fresh air; I couldn't sleep. Through these difficult times, God encouraged me that "suffering produces perseverance; perseverance, character; and character, hope" (Romans 5:3-4).

Persistent prayer, a positive attitude and a sense of humor are essential for a good marriage. When I laugh at myself and trust God's provision, I have hope for days ahead. I can choose to complain and give in to bitterness, or I can ask God for help to forgive, respect and love.

Contrary to predictions of failure from family and friends, Fred and I will soon be celebrating our fortieth anniversary! We continue to discover new differences, but Jesus is our balance. He is our strength when we're weak, our hope for overwhelming days, our power and wisdom to overcome any struggles. When we see life through our own perspectives alone and daily challenges fall on us like rain, God's loving umbrella will shelter us, prosper our love and bring His harmony.

> *Lord, thank You for Your encouragement and power, enabling me to be victorious in challenging times. You pour Your love into my heart. Help me to forgive and then begin again. Amen.*

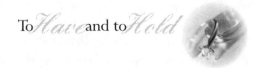
Living by the Lord's Prayer

Lydia Harris

And forgive us our debts, as we forgive our debtors. (Matthew 6:12, KJV)

I had memorized the Lord's Prayer from the Bible as a child and recited it during church services. I even sang it as a solo. Although I knew it by heart, applying it was another matter.

While my husband and I attended a marriage conference, he did something that upset me. I slipped into bed that night, built an invisible wall between us and hugged my side of the bed. Icy silence replaced our usual friendly chit-chat.

Restless and unable to sleep, I prayed, "God, what does my husband need from me?"

"Unconditional love," came the quick prompting from the Holy Spirit.

"No! He doesn't deserve it," I inwardly snapped and fumed in silence.

Although I knew the Bible taught that I should forgive my husband, I wasn't ready to do so. I'd rather stay angry a while longer. Besides, he should apologize first!

As I lay awake, silently rehashing my husband's bad behavior and justifying mine, God's Spirit pricked my conscience. He reminded me of my own faults and of how often my husband forgives me instead of harboring a grudge. Gradually my thinking shifted from blaming my husband to examining myself. I sensed the enormity of my sins and the high price Jesus paid for my forgiveness. If God could forgive me for so many sins, couldn't I forgive my husband for one small matter?

Finally my hard heart softened, and I obeyed God's prompting. I rolled over, gently tapped my husband on the shoulder, and said, "Honey, my attitude was wrong. Will you forgive me?"

"Yes, dear. I'm sorry too. Will you forgive me?"

The wall crumbled! We hugged and then slept peacefully. Once again I was reminded of the saying, "A happy marriage is the union of two good forgivers."

Lord God, thank You for Your forgiveness. When we confess our sins, You are faithful and just to forgive and cleanse us (see 1 John 1:9, KJV). Help me forgive my husband and others the way You have forgiven me. Amen.

An Ornament of
Blown Glass Called "Trust"

Brenda Hendricks

I urge you to live a life worthy of the calling you have received. Be completely humble and gentle; be patient, bearing with one another in love. Make every effort to keep the unity of the Spirit through the bond of peace. (Ephesians 4:1-3)

"Honey, can we please stop there?" I pleaded with my sweet new husband.

The Corning Glass Factory in Corning, New York, is not listed as one of the top ten most desired stops for honeymooners in any of the modern bridal magazines, but I have always been fascinated by the art of glassblowing.

Of course his reply was, "Certainly, dear, if we can stop at the fish hatchery on the way!"

After we viewed the fish, we arrived at the factory. The master of the art of glassblowing amazed us. He twisted and twirled the blow tube as he blew, and the intricate ornament developed. Then his knowledgeable hands performed the ticklish operation of removing the fragile ornament from the blow tube. The artist gingerly set his masterpiece aside to finish cooling.

God has created people with intricate adornments which are as fragile as blown glass. Developing trust in personal relationships is one of the most delicate of all. It is a sheer, beautiful, hollow vessel in which we carry our love and respect for others. Trust must be handled with the utmost care.

The interesting thing about trust is that we do not carry our own vessels. Instead, we bear the vessels of those around us, especially our spouses. If trust is fragmented, it is next to impossible to repair. Lies are the most damaging to trust, so we need to carry the trust of others with the gentle but firm hands of truth. Suspicions and false accusations are just as injurious as lies. We can mar our own trust, which someone else is holding, by allowing our suspicions to squeeze our vessels until they shatter. Trust is easily destroyed! Once this intricate vessel of trust is broken, the love and respect it carried seeps away.

Once, in the heat of an argument, my husband announced, "I am telling you the truth. It is up to you to believe it or not. I can't do anything about that."

Although my husband tried to handle my delicate vessel of trust with care, I had not allowed it. I decided to put it in Jesus' hands— it is much safer there. My husband earned my trust through his honesty. In the meantime, Jesus gave me peace of mind.

If our vessel is damaged or even shattered, Jesus is the only one who can repair it. He can also replenish the love and respect that has seeped away.

> *Dear Lord, help us to be very cautious while handling these tender vessels of trust that our loved ones have committed to us. May we always hold them with the same care with which we desire our trust bearers to handle ours. In Jesus' name, Amen.*

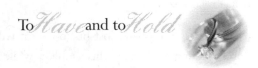

Out of Touch

Gail Black Kopf

Thy right hand hath holden me up, and thy gentleness hath made me great. (Psalm 18:35, KJV)

"You still hold hands?" said my observant neighbor with a tinge of disbelief in her voice. "After thirty years of marriage?"

"Why, yes," I replied. "Don't you?"

She sadly shook her head. It definitely wasn't the time to tell her that my husband and I usually showered together. After she left, I realized anew how important the gift of touch is. It often expresses our concern and interest more effectively than verbal communication.

I thought back to the time when my mammogram revealed a suspicious lump in my left breast. Despite my best efforts, I was anxious and fearful through an ultrasound, then a needle aspiration. In the crowded waiting room afterward, my husband held my hand, thus conveying not only his love but his understanding and willingness to help. We embraced each other when the test for cancer was negative.

Phyllis K. Davis, in *The Power of Touch,* states, "Without touch a baby dies, the human heart aches, and the soul withers." Medical research has proven that touch has a therapeutic value; it is necessary for both emotional and physical well-being.

The day my husband lost his job, I sat with him on the front porch, resting my head on his shoulder while the dark clouds of a summer storm, like our latest crisis, gathered momentum. Later, planning a job search and reorganizing our finances would enter the picture, but at that moment he needed a comforting, soothing touch to help assuage his grief and disappointment.

Since physical closeness is an essential of marriage, it's imperative that couples nurture this part of their relationships on a daily basis. "Reach out and touch someone," the popular motto of a telephone company, makes good sense.

Today, why not put your arm around your spouse's shoulder, give him an unexpected hug or try holding hands as you watch television or take a walk together? Not only will it give you both a warm, secure feeling, but it will build true closeness and trust—the basis for a satisfying marriage.

Heavenly Father, help me to pass along Your loving touch to others. Amen.

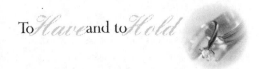

"Hold Me"

Barbara Hibschman

And you husbands must be loving and kind to your wives. (Colossians 3:19, TLB)

He has every right to be upset and disappointed with me, I thought as I made my way up the stairs to our second-floor apartment with the car antenna in hand.

"Where have you been?" Jim asked. Staring at the antenna, he realized I had been in an accident. "Are you hurt? I've been so worried about you."

I tried to explain and burst into tears. Jim didn't question or blame me but instead just held me close until I stopped sobbing. His embrace was so assuring, comforting and accepting.

"Traffic was horrible," I said. "As I was following bumper-to-bumper at about five miles per hour, I bumped the car in front of me. I didn't think there was any damage, so I failed to get out of the car to check it out. The car followed me when I got off the expressway. The driver honked, yelled and made obscene gestures at me. I pulled over and stopped. He was so angry he got out and hit the hood of my car with his fists and swore at me. He said I should have stopped and that I am like all the other young women in this generation: irresponsible.

"When I immediately apologized and took responsibility for not getting out of the car, he calmed down a bit. Then I got out and took a look. There wasn't even a scratch or any indication that we had bumped.

"I tried to reason with him. I said, 'Sir, the cars are fine. We are fine. Please accept my apology for not stopping.' He was so angry that he got back into his car and took off in a rage.

"As I got back into my car, I prayed for help. Psalm 46:1-2 came to mind where it says, 'God is our refuge and strength, an ever-present help in trouble. Therefore we will not fear.' "

"You're safe now," Jim said. "You'll be fine. So how did the antenna get broken?"

"I stopped to get the mail. I didn't notice how close I was to our mailbox. I hit it, and all the others are attached, so there are sixteen slanting mailboxes!"

"Well, I guess we'll get to know our neighbors," Jim teased as he held me close.

Jim's response to my failures and fears was a picture of God caring with unconditional love. He was so patient and kind. God too embraces us and holds us steady through His Word.

There are unexpected happenings that come into our lives that could rip our oneness apart. Acceptance and forgiveness of each other and ourselves are the glue that holds us together when the pressures of life rage against us.

> *Heavenly Father, help us to hold one another in times of failure and fear. Thank You for helping, holding and strengthening us through Your Word. We are safe, for we are in the arms of our Beloved. Amen.*

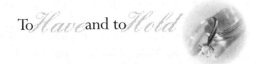

Christ over All

Eva Marie Everson

I will set him over my house and my kingdom forever; his throne will be established forever. (1 Chronicles 17:14)

I shocked my husband of twenty-three years when I asked, "How can I be a better wife?"—but no more than I shocked myself.

I'd been reading Watchman Nee's book *God's Overcomers*, in which he states that everything God has done has been in order to set His Son as Lord over all. I'd pondered those words, realizing that while Christ *should* be on the throne in my marriage, more times than not, *I am!* In order to correct this, I decided to ask my husband how I might be a better spouse.

Dennis began with a few honest suggestions, but the third one threw me for a loop. "I'm sick of seeing you in those overall shorts all the time!"

My cute little overalls? "But they're so comfortable," I argued, taking Christ right off His throne. "Surely you don't expect me to dress as though I'm heading for a downtown office."

"No. Just something besides those overalls."

When I'd finished pouting, I ran for the phone. "This calls for shopping!" I declared to my best friend, who insisted she could meet me in a New York minute.

Naturally I found absolutely *nothing* that suited my "at home" tastes. After several hours, I decided to give up. I sighed. Either I would dress uncomfortably to please my man or he would have to see me in overalls when he walked in the door at the end of a hard day. I wondered where all this stood with the whole "Christ on the throne" thing.

I headed toward the escalators. Suddenly a shock of leopard print caught my eye and I turned. There was the lingerie department, filled to overflowing with pajama sets designed as loungewear. I spun around and headed toward satin. An hour later I was in my car with four PJ sets.

When Dennis walked in the door that afternoon, I met him in my new flowing attire. "Wow!" he said.

"Compromise," I said. "I'll wear my overalls during the day, but from evening time on, I'll dress to thrill. Deal?"

We sealed it with a kiss. It's a little thing, I know. Yet I can say without blinking that my willingness to dress in a more flattering way went a long way toward pleasing my husband . . . and I pray a long way toward making Christ Lord . . . *over all*!

Sweet Jesus, as we learn to bend toward pleasing others, help us to elevate You to a place of honor in our lives, in our homes and in our marriages—by the power of Your Spirit. Amen.

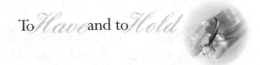

Oil and Water

Earlene D. Benson

*For this reason a man will leave his father and mother . . . and they
will become one flesh.* (Genesis 2:24)

"It will never work!" "You have nothing in common!" "Oil and
water just won't mix!" friends said in reaction to the announce-
ment of my coming marriage.

In a way they were right. Norm and I had nothing in common.
He and I came from different worlds. He was of the fourth generation born and raised on the family farm in central New York State. I
was born in Ohio, spent my childhood near Buffalo and in the last
eight years had lived in five different cities. To him "home" was a
twelve-room house surrounded by 500 acres of corn, hay, oats and
cows. To me "home" meant wherever I unpacked my suitcase.

My life was teaching, plays, concerts, writing and literary
groups. Norm's life was farming. The little spare time he had was
taken up in church activities and farm meetings. He didn't know
a quatrain from a sonnet, and I couldn't tell the difference between a Hereford and a Holstein.

"Well," I replied to my critics, "at least we'll have a lot to
teach each other. Marriage is, after all, a learning experience."

Over time I have lost track of those friends. It's too bad. I
would like to tell them that our marriage has worked very well
for over fifty years. We have four children and seven grandchil-

dren in common. As for oil and water, any cook can tell you they will mix very well. All you need is the right binder. What flour can do for gravy, Christ can do for marriage.

Dear Lord, thank You for binding our hearts together to make us one in You. Amen.

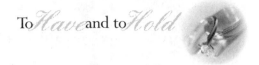

Hearing His Heart

Amy Givler

*Two people can accomplish more than twice as much as one; they get a
better return for their labor. If one person falls, the other can reach out
and help. But people who are alone when they fall are in real trouble.*
(Ecclesiastes 4:9-10, NLT)

When Don stepped through the kitchen door that November
evening, I noticed his forehead was furrowed. "James has cancer," he said. He and James worked at the same state-run hospital, sharing the workload with eight other physicians.

I went to Don and buried my head in his shoulder. "How awful," I murmured. Don and I both loved James—and his wife,
Jenny, too. How were they handling this blow?

"He's getting surgery tomorrow," Don said as I sat on a stool.
"He'll be out for at least six weeks. It's going to be tough. We were
already short one doctor, and now we're short two. There's no one
to take up the slack. I don't think I can work any harder than I am
already."

I stared at him, startled. *How can Don be thinking of himself and his
workload at a time like this? What about James? He's the one with cancer*, I
thought. But now Don was staring out the window, his shoulders
slumped. I bit my lip to keep sarcastic words from tumbling out.

I remember, when I first met Don, being attracted by his selfless-
ness and compassion. Eighteen years of marriage later, I knew those

qualities were genuine. So where was this self-centered streak coming from?

Silently I got dinner ready. Early the next morning, during my quiet time with God, I was praying for James when Don's words came rushing back. "I don't think I can work any harder than I am already." Why hadn't I been able to hear what he was really saying?

Now I could see beyond his words to his pain. Far from being selfish, he was warning me about how difficult the next few months would be. Hadn't he also been inviting me to come alongside him and help carry the heavy burden he was staggering under? Who else knew how hard he was already working, how close he was to the breaking point? Only me—yet I had trivialized his pain.

How many times over the years had I just wanted Don's listening ear—his support—and he had given it gladly? Now a chance to return that favor had come, but I'd missed it. "Forgive me, Lord," I prayed. And before he left for work, I asked Don to forgive me too. He did.

"Please keep telling me what you're thinking and how you're feeling," I added. "I'm listening now."

Lord, help me know when my husband needs a friend, not a critic. If he comes to me with a problem, give me the grace to stay silent until I have Your insight into the situation and can speak words of love. Amen.

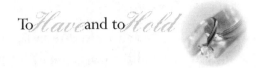

He Called Me "Susan"

Sue Cameron

He calls his own sheep by name and leads them out. (John 10:3)

My husband, Craig, and I frequently use nicknames when addressing each other. Craig often makes up a name for me that rhymes with the last word in the sentence he is speaking. So he might say, "You're cute, little dute." Our current favorites are Huzzie and Wommie.

Of all the names Craig has ever called me, there is only one time that he called me by my proper legal name of Susan. I gave up that name and became Sue sometime around seventh grade when I was trying to figure out who I was. But there was one time, one very significant time, when he sternly said, "Susan!"

Labor is one of those things that you really don't know much about until you've experienced it. I decided I wanted to have natural childbirth. After all, I figured that if women in far-off rice paddies could have a baby in the morning and go back to work in the afternoon, then I should be able to handle it. So, during my first pregnancy, I read books, ate healthy food, exercised daily and attended weekly classes to prepare for natural childbirth.

Then I went into labor. Somewhere around transition, which is the hardest part of the birthing process, I decided I had really misjudged things. I was doing everything I'd been told to do and I still hurt more than I'd ever hurt before. Suddenly those women in far-off countries were really far off. They had nothing to do with me and the contractions that gripped my body. I couldn't relax. I didn't want to breathe "hee, hee, hee, ha" anymore. I was ready to stop the roller coaster and get off the ride!

So when the next contraction hit, I gave in to it, letting it carry me wherever it wanted. I wound up in a place of panic. I squeezed my eyes shut, screamed and arched my back as the power of the contractions took control of me. I felt lost, as if I was sinking down, down, down. Then, into that darkness, I heard someone shout my name, "Susan!" The voice was full of authority and love, demanding my full attention, refusing to be ignored.

I opened my eyes. My young husband stood directly above me, his face inches from mine. He gripped my shoulders and peered deep into my eyes. "Susan!" he repeated. "Breathe—hee, hee, hee, ha."

Suddenly, I wasn't drowning anymore; there was someone who loved me who was right there to take my hand and lead me through the deep waters, to help me keep my head up, to remind me to breathe. When I obeyed his voice, I found I was safe once again.

Huzzie—I mean, Craig—has never again called me "Susan." There has been no need. But I learned in that moment that a stern voice is often the very anchor I need when the storms of life threaten to undo me.

> *Thank You, Father, that in marriage we speak to each other in many ways. Thank You that Craig knew when to use a stern voice with me and that You still use him to say true things to me that are hard to hear. Amen.*

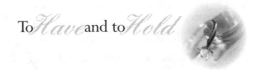

To Hold or Not to Hold

Mary D. Smith

Love is patient and kind. (1 Corinthians 13:4, RSV)

During the winter of 1988, painful childhood memories had begun to float to the surface of my consciousness. I could hold them down no longer. They rose like bubbles in a foamy sea. Suddenly my paranoia and my unreasonable fears began to make sense.

During the next three years, I remembered episode after episode of being molested. And each time, my husband, Sam, would comfort me as terror and helplessness gushed from my soul.

I told Sam how my abuser had filled a laundry tub and forced my head under the water because I refused to do what he wanted. How he took me out to the woods and abandoned me for hours, saying he would leave me there forever if I told anyone. How he made me watch him molest my baby sister. Sam listened to these accounts and more pour from my lips.

During those three years, I hated for anyone to touch me. And anyone included my husband! Unfair as it was to Sam, most nights I would feel compelled to wrap myself in my blue flannel nightgown and sleep perched on the edge of our queen-sized bed. Sometimes I would stay awake all night, finally falling asleep on the couch at 3 a.m.

Through all those years Sam reassured me, telling me I was not dirty and corrupted and defiled—my abuser was.

I had no idea how remarkable Sam's behavior was until one day when I talked with my counselor. "I want to meet this man," she said. "Do you understand how wonderful he is?"

I'm ashamed to say I took Sam for granted. *He should be nice to me*, I reasoned. *After all, I was a victim.*

While asking forgiveness from Sam, I began to understand that I had done the same thing to Christ. How often had I said, "Stay away, Lord. Don't touch me"? How often did prayers flow from my mouth until I was drained of emotion? Then I would refuse to let Jesus bind my wounds. And when Jesus comforted me with a sunset, a flower or a sweet kiss from a child, how often did I take Him for granted? "You should do this and more, God," I said. "After all, I was a victim."

Sam and I just celebrated our twenty-third wedding anniversary. And as for that blue flannel nightie—I rarely wear it anymore.

> *Please, Lord, help us never to take You for granted. Help us to trust You with our deepest hurts, our foulest betrayals, our heaviest grief. And please forgive us when we cannot. Thank You for Your patience and kindness. Amen.*

Butterflies, Rocks
and Opposites

Tina Krause

There are different kinds of service, but the same Lord. (1 Corinthians 12:5)

"Fine, I'm leaving!" I yelled, slamming the door behind me. Fuming, I sat on the back deck stairs and glared across the yard. "Lord, I've had it," I snarled. "We just aren't on the same wavelength."

Jim and I were young Christians attempting to work out the problems of a shaky marriage. We were complete opposites: I, flighty and emotional; Jim, silent and intense. I read all of the latest books on marriage, but a Total Woman I was not. And Jim was less than the image of the perfect pastor with whom I had hoped to share my life.

My husband's lack of spiritual fervor concerned me. He was less evangelistic, less outwardly "spiritual" than I, which magnified the conflicts and widened the gap between us.

"How can two Christians who love You differ and argue so much?" I questioned. "And why can't Jim see how wrong he is?" While mumbling my complaints to God, I noticed a brilliant-colored butterfly flutter past, dipping and swooping in all directions. At first its movements reminded me of my own. Anxiously

I had flittered in every direction, busying myself in the "work of the Lord" while, from my perspective, Jim barely penetrated his spiritual cocoon.

Blinded to my husband's spiritual gifts, I pleaded with God in self-righteous tones. "Lord, stir Jim within and make him a powerhouse for You so that both of us can serve You together."

Again the monarch butterfly landed on a smooth, gray rock and, for a moment, rested. The sun's rays reflected off its stilled wings. This time its colors radiated more brightly than before as God silenced my sanctimonious thoughts.

"You are a butterfly, but Jim is a rock," God whispered to my spirit. "Rest on the abilities and wisdom I have imparted to him."

The Scripture from the book of Corinthians suddenly came alive as I began to see that God dispenses dissimilar gifts to butterflies and rocks, and each one is of equal importance in the kingdom of God. The air that had soured with hostility moments before filled with the peace of the Holy Spirit. God grounded my butterfly wings on the spiritual head of my "rock" husband, and the healing began.

Thirty-two years later, our differences have transformed into a ministry of love, appreciation and devotion for one another and for our Lord. And each day I am reminded that "to have and to hold" requires a mutual respect, admiration and appreciation for rocks as well as for butterflies.

Dear Lord, thank You for the bond of love and harmony this butterfly and rock share. Through better and worse, we possess the highest respect and appreciation for one another despite our differences, all because of Your sustaining love. Amen.

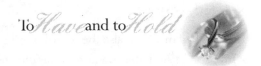

On the Wings of Truth

Kathleen Swartz McQuaig

Then you will know the truth, and the truth will set you free. (John 8:32)

Fatigue crept into every corner of my weary body. Idly I thumbed through the mail, still distracted by the concerned faces of the adults I'd tutored that day—concerns that had more to do with keeping jobs than comprehending lessons.

Mentally I willed myself to shift gears for two active teenagers who would soon be at my side. My head pounded; my muscles ached. I noted the piles of papers strewn across the dining room table and turned away. Exhausted, I sank into a comfy chair by the window and stretched my legs onto the ottoman for some much-needed rest. It had been a long day.

Moments later I heard the rattling of my husband's keys at our front door. Tossing aside the throw pillows that I'd just positioned under my arms, I jumped up. Defying weariness, I quickly busied myself with the unsightly stacks on the dining room table. By the time Scott closed the front door and climbed the stairs, he found me industriously sorting through a pile of papers.

Honesty? The absurdity of the scene took a minute to register. It wasn't Scott who needed me to appear productive, but me. I was the keeper of a mental "should do" list longer than my arm. I was the one who expected more of myself than any one person would dare to ask of me. I was also the one who believed honesty to be one of my greatest strengths. And now I was the one staring at the hands feigning productivity.

I realized in that instant that it is not the things we say, but the little things that we do, that often tell the biggest lies.

I looked at this man with whom I'd built a relationship on trust and truth. We'd shared almost twenty years of marriage, the joys and challenges of parenting our teens and the blessing of our newest child on the way. How could I have let unrealistic expectations cloud the truth?

Sheepishly I met Scott's eyes above my fumbling hands and stopped shuffling papers. I felt foolish at my attempted cover-up, but as I confessed the truth, we broke into broad smiles, laughing at ourselves.

For me, in that moment, honesty was redefined—action included.

As Scott held out his arms in a hug, a new freedom surged inside me. Then we both sat down for some much-needed rest.

> *Lord, help us soar with wings of truth, relating honestly to each other in all we say and do. And thank You for helping us realize how wonderful those much-needed Sabbath moments can be. Amen.*

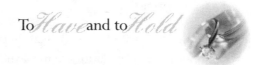
Snuggling Up to the Lord
Janet Packard

When we remember you on our bed, we meditate on you in the night
watches. For you have been our help, and in the shadow of your wings
we sing for joy. Our soul clings to you; your right hand upholds us.
(Psalm 63:6-8, author's paraphrase)

Our walnut, Danish-modern, forty-four-year-old double bed has been the place for much holding over the years. Although too large to fit into my hope chest, the bed came with me when I married Milton forty-three years ago. The springs and mattress have been replaced, but the sharp corners are still a hazard. Because of middle-age spread, the bed has shrunk. Smaller, however, means cozier.

As our children approached the teen years, family devotions became more difficult and no longer seemed adequate. In bed—sometimes at night, other times early in the morning—with our arms wrapped around each other, Milton and I prayed for our teenagers. First one would speak, then the other—back and forth, like a conversation. We sensed the Lord directing our thoughts and giving us new insights. He held us as we held each other.

We had many concerns, as varied as our three children's personalities. Our oldest child threatened to leave home when he reached eighteen even though he had not yet graduated from high school. Our second son took up the habit of smoking. At times our daughter faced danger while in high school and college. All three dealt with financial needs in college. We encountered morality issues, including homosexuality. Our teenager's friend shocked him by stating he was gay and then attempted suicide in our son's presence.

Prayer is what kept us functioning as a couple and as parents. When a crisis hit, fear took over. But after praying, God's peace washed over us as we acknowledged that He cared and was working "all things together for good."

Because we serve a gracious and mighty God, all three children married Christians and are seeking the Lord's wisdom as they raise their children to follow Christ. Because we have added three spouses and six grandchildren to our prayer list, we have even more reason to snuggle up to the Lord. He continues to provide wisdom and direction.

> *Thank You, Father, for my Christian mate to have and to hold. When we cling to You, You cling to us and give comfort. Thank You for the power of prayer and for Your all-wise counsel. Amen.*

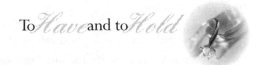

Then and Now

Betty J. Johnson

Many waters cannot quench the flame of love, neither can the floods drown it. If a man tried to buy it with everything he owned, he couldn't do it. (Song of Solomon 8:7, TLB)

Forty-four years ago our honeymoon destination was a sleepy little town nestled in the Ozark Mountains. Recently we returned for an anniversary trip down memory lane and found a thriving metropolis known to the world as Branson, Missouri.

In the late 1950s, traveling to another state was as unfamiliar to us as being married was. It was exciting, glamorous and adventuresome. Now, as a seasoned traveler, I casually nudged my husband's arm and commented, "Looks like spring is here. See those gorgeous pink tulips and yellow daffodils?" Often we only nudge and point or smile and understand unspoken words.

Back then, I snuggled close to my new husband in the '54 Desoto. (After all, I "belonged" on his side of the bench seat for all the world to see!) We laughed and planned our new life together. Now in our Ford Taurus with the individual seats, we're two comfortable companions. He drives; I knit and ask questions like, "What shall we serve when the whole family is home for Easter?" or "When do our grandson's baseball games start?"

Then we found a mom-and-pop motel just off the main street that overlooked a winding creek. We could hear the water gurgling as it meandered by our window. Now the Hyatts, Holiday Inns and Sheratons compete for our business, and my husband suggests, "This traffic and noise is too much. Let's find a quiet cabin near the lake."

Then, as though life couldn't be enjoyed without us being together every second of every minute of every hour of every day, we never left each other's sides. Now I sit on the cabin deck, enjoying my favorite hobby—reading—while my graying hubby stands by the water (100 yards away) enjoying his favorite hobby—fishing. He turns and waves. I wave back and sigh. "Life is good. Thank You, Lord."

Then we didn't ruminate about change. Now we ponder the astronomical changes that have taken place in our lives, and he comments, "Can you believe this town could change so much in forty-four years?"

"Well, think how much our bodies have changed," I laughingly respond.

We sit quietly for a moment, then I wonder aloud, "Do you think that God has an unchanging plan for marriage?"

"I believe it has to do with listening," my wise husband answers. "It's about listening to each other and listening to God. And it's also about adjusting to life's changes," he adds.

Forty-four years ago we focused on our love for each other and the exciting days ahead. Now he reaches for my hand, raises it to his lips and says, "I still love you, honey."

Forty-four years ago, we were young and full of dreams. Now we're young at heart and full of cherished memories.

Father, when I feel the world changing and I become frightened, remind me of Your unchanging love for each of us. Give me ears to hear Your voice and the voice of my spouse. May I respond with love and obedience. Amen.

On a Mountaintop in Norway

Charlotte Adelsperger

Trust in the LORD with all your heart and lean not on your own understanding; in all your ways acknowledge him, and he will make your paths straight. (Proverbs 3:5-6)

In 1961 I experienced the exciting adventure of being in Norway where I attended the University of Oslo International Summer School. I was an American fresh out of college and a beginning teacher back in the States.

One weekend my travel friend, Karin Lindahl, and I took a train trip from Oslo to the coastal town of Bergen. We rode Bergen's funicular, or mountain cable car, to the top of Mount Fløyen that overlooks the city. What an awesome view of the harbor and fjords! While Karin shopped, I ambled down a path to a quiet spot. To my surprise, an inner ache surfaced. *Will I ever find a good husband?*

That night I wrote in my diary about my time alone on that mountain path on July 21, 1961: "Today on Fløyen, I came to a lovely place where I saw rich moss among the trees. I spent time in silent prayer. I opened my whole self to God and asked Him to guide my life as a Christian single person and teacher. As I prayed I turned over to God my deepest desire—to find the husband right for me.

"May I always remember the serenity and power on the mountain overlooking Bergen," I wrote. "Today was a day of dedication."

After I returned to the States, I dated several prospective mates, but none seemed to be "the one." I became discouraged.

Three years later, when I was teaching in the Kansas City suburbs, I attended a singles event at a church. There I met Bob Adelsperger, recently back from Air Force service on Okinawa. Now there was a Christian man with qualities! We dated, fell in love and were married in June 1965.

Our love grew stronger through the years. Often I thought back on my time of prayer on a mountaintop in Norway. I could see how it made all the difference to surrender my heart's desires to the Lord. Of course, I told Bob about my mountain prayer—and how God led me to him!

When Bob and I planned a trip to Europe for 1998, we included Norway. We traveled the same scenic train route to Bergen. As we took the funicular to the top of Mount Fløyen on a sunny June afternoon, I could feel my heart speeding up.

"Come this way," I urged, tugging his hand. "I'm taking you to the spot where I prayed. It may take a few minutes to find it— considering that was thirty-seven years ago!" But there it was, lovely view and all! And thick moss still covered the ground. Bob and I were all smiles as a Norwegian snapped our picture. We hugged.

"I thank God for you," I whispered. Then we kissed, and the camera clicked again.

Almighty God, thank You for Your creative faithfulness when I turn my heart's desires over to You. May I trust You even more! Through Christ, Amen.

Unexpected Blessings

Sharon Gibson

And when we obey him, every path he guides us on is fragrant with his lovingkindness and his truth. (Psalm 25:10, TLB)

"I think the Lord is telling me that we need to take Robert in and take care of him."

"Well, I don't hear Him saying that!" I replied fearfully.

Sixteen-year-old Robert had been abandoned on the ranch where my husband directed a program for recovering alcohol and drug abusers from Skid Row, Los Angeles. One of the men in the recovery program, with tears in his eyes, begged my husband to find a home for Robert. "If you don't, he will end up like me—in jail and then on the streets. Please do something!"

After a month of praying and searching for a home for Robert, my husband sensed the Lord telling us to care for him. I couldn't see it! Although I had never been able to have kids and desperately wanted them, I questioned starting motherhood at age forty-one with a troubled teenager. Additionally, I was battling chronic fatigue. I just didn't feel up to it.

As I sought the Lord, I remembered something He told me years earlier. "I will lead you through your husband." During a "prodigal daughter" period of my life I had married Stan. When the Lord spoke that word to me, Stan had been going to church with me for only a year. At the time I questioned Him. I had been raised by missionary parents, went to Bible school and did extensive Bible study on my own. I couldn't imagine how the Lord could lead me through someone who was "so much less knowledgeable" about Christianity, but over the years the Lord had done just that. I had seen Stan grow in his faith and his trust in the Lord. But now I was faced with a challenge that defied logic! After much thought and struggling, I finally said, "You know, Lord, if this is Your will, then even if it is hard, there is a blessing that I don't want to miss."

I agreed to take Robert in. Later, through my husband's leadership, we adopted three additional abandoned and abused teenagers, this time from Brazil and Colombia.

The challenges of relating to teens with deep emotional wounds, combined with cultural and language differences, are oftentimes intense. It could have broken our marriage apart; instead it brought forth our strengths. Stan is strict and good at setting boundaries. I am nurturing and adept at conflict resolution. The children and I need his boundaries, and he and the children welcome my compassion and tender heart. We both recognize that we could not do this without that balance. This has caused us to value each other to a greater degree.

Can I trust the Lord in my husband's leadership? So far, he has a pretty good track record!

Lord, thank You for giving me the wisdom to obey You and for the gift of children I dearly love. Continue to help me to humble myself and to yield to my husband's leadership. Help me to trust You even when it doesn't make sense and to never forget that when we obey You our deepest desires are fulfilled. Amen.

When He Doesn't Believe

Virelle Kidder

Your beauty should . . . be . . . the unfading beauty of a gentle and
quiet spirit, which is of great worth in God's sight. (1 Peter 3:3-4)

"What's for lunch?" Steve mumbled, barely looking up from the couch. There sat my husband, unshaven, still in his bathrobe, watching a ball game on TV. He looked just as bad as he had two hours earlier when four-year-old Lauren and I had left for church, only now he was hungry. Out to the kitchen I went, and with a loud banging of pots and pans, I slapped together a colorless meal.

Without a doubt, we were miserable! Steve had no interest in my new faith in Christ. In fact, he felt like I had taken a lover. As he retreated into a hostile, quiet shell, I grew increasingly hurt and resentful, casting disapproving glances at everything he did.

We sat down like inmates, and I said a stiff prayer over dinner. When Steve looked up, he asked, "How was church?"

"It was wonderful," I returned flatly. "You might have liked it if you'd been there." Another disapproving glance.

"I don't think so. I don't fit in there," he answered thoughtfully. After a long pause he added, "You know, if I were you, I'd feel guilty."

"Guilty? Guilty?" I exploded, bringing my fist down hard on the table. Lauren darted out of the room. This was too much. Entirely uncalled for. "Why should I feel guilty? You're the one who's rejected Christ! You're the one who refuses to believe! How can you have the nerve to say that?"

And with the softest words I had ever heard, Steve directed his hazel eyes at mine and delivered a blow I would never recover from: "Because, Virelle, I am a pagan, and I'm behaving exactly like a pagan should behave, but you are a Christian, and you are not loving."

Silence. For once I had no words.

Later, on my knees in our bedroom, I cried out to God. "Lord, Steve can't possibly be right, can he? You know how hard I've tried to grow as a Christian. I've done everything, Lord. You don't think I'm unloving too, do You?"

Silence again, and I knew that God agreed with Steve. Having received His complete forgiveness and unconditional love in Christ, could I justify not offering the same love to Steve? At that moment, I knew I had to change, and radically at that.

It's been more than twenty-five years since that day. I have learned that in God's household, love is the power that transforms. Now I marvel at the awesome Christian man Steve has become, far more wonderful than I had dreamed. His strong but gentle spiritual leadership has given our family and many others a wonderful model of both the tenderness and energy of God's love that releases us to become all He wants us to be. Our shared joy is found in building up other marriages and families through small groups, teaching, speaking and writing together.

This year marks our thirtieth anniversary. Has it all been smooth sailing? Certainly not, but it has been an exciting and humbling journey learning to love one another and move forward as a team.

Father, help me trust You when my prayers seem unanswered but are not, and season my words with the graciousness and love that only comes from You. Amen.

[Excerpted from an article with the same title that was first printed in the March/April 2001 issue of *Today's Christian Woman*. Used by permission of the author, Virelle Kidder.]

When One Became Two

Michele T. Huey

Neither was man created for woman, but woman for man. (1 Corinthians 11:9)

"It is not good for you to be alone," said the Lord God to the man. "I will make a helper suitable for you."

"But what about my dog?" the man asked. "He keeps me pretty good company. Or my horse? Or the parakeet?"

"They may keep you company," said the Lord, "but I think you need something more."

"What more could I want?" the man asked. "The dog wags his tail and licks my face when he sees me, the horse nuzzles up to me when I have a carrot for him and the parakeet keeps it from getting too quiet around here."

"I have something better in mind for you," said the Lord.

"What could be better than warm, wet kisses from a furry dog who stays right at my feet, even when I'm sleeping?" asked the man.

To make His point, the Lord brought all the beasts of the field and all the birds of the air to the man. But none could help him tend the garden, encourage him when he made a mistake, cuddle with him in the cool hours before dawn or hug him after a hard day. Not one could pack his lunch, rub his back or pull out the thorn from the bottom of his foot.

But the man still insisted his dog was a fine companion.

He doesn't understand because he doesn't know anything different, thought the Lord. *I'll just have to show him.* So the Lord God caused the man to fall into a deep sleep. Taking one of the man's ribs, He formed another being similar to, but different than, the man. When the man woke up, he instantly recognized that, unlike the dog or the horse or the bird, this beautiful creature was part of him. Without her, he would never again be complete.

"At last!" he cried. "Bone of my bone and flesh of my flesh!" He called her "woman" because it sounded like his own name—man.

"Listen up," said the Lord. "Although I made her especially for you, she is part of you, and you must take as good care of her as you do your own body. You must love her as you love yourself. She is strong, but you must protect her. She is hardy, but you must handle her with tenderness. Love her, but also cherish her. Treat her like she's the queen of your world. Do this," said the Lord, "and she will not only be your helper, your lover, your other half . . . she will be your friend."

Thank You, Lord, for the life-companion you have made just for me. Amen.

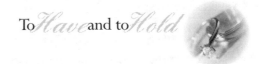

Dropping Everything

Susan A.J. Lyttek

In this same way, husbands ought to love their wives as their own bodies. He who loves his wife loves himself. After all, no one ever hated his own body, but he feeds and cares for it, just as Christ does the church. (Ephesians 5:28-29)

Psychologists say we learn what marriage is from our parents. My parents, as a rule, are not demonstrative in their affections. Even so, I was convinced at a young age that they loved each other dearly. An unlisted phone number is proof to this day that my father loves my mother as much as he does himself.

Shortly after we moved and I had started school, the prank calls began. They unnerved my mother, but she believed in keeping a straight backbone and a logical mind, so she determined to ignore them. She did so until one day when the caller said he had my father and threatened to kill him. He sounded so believable that my logical mother lost control. It was the only time I can remember seeing her cry.

She called my dad's employer and eventually succeeded in reaching my father, who assured her nothing was wrong. When he heard what had happened, he left work early and came home. When Dad walked through the door, I thought Mom would never stop hugging him.

Then my father, the man my sisters and I affectionately call "cheap," called the telephone company and asked for an unlisted number. Was he aware, they asked, that it would increase his monthly bill? He was, and he insisted on their changing the number as soon as possible.

And through that event, one little girl was assured that her father loved her mother very much.

> *Thank You, Lord, for the husbands and fathers who love their wives with fierce devotion, and that in a country torn by divorce there are still lifetime marriages. Help us to learn from their examples. Help us obey the truth in Your instructions. In Christ's name we pray, Amen.*

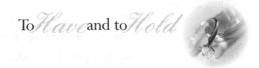

A Commitment to Prayer

Jim Russell

Rejoice always, pray without ceasing, in everything give thanks; for this is the will of God in Christ Jesus for you. (1 Thessalonians 5:16-18, NKJV)

In the years before ours became an "empty nest," in those exciting moments before leaving on vacation, we gathered as a family and prayed—my precious wife, Phyllis; myself; and our children, Kathy, Vicki, Lori, Jimmy and Amy. We thanked our heavenly Father for family, vacation time and the weekly rental lake shore cottage. We asked for a safe trip, good weather and joyful togetherness. We prayed we would get along in harmony and be kind to one another.

Years later, while doing research for a book, Phyllis and I discovered how important and meaningful those family prayer moments were in the hearts, minds and lives of our children. To lead the family in audible prayer presents a parent as surrendered, submissive and obedient to the highest Authority. It is a powerful lesson by example, not lost on the hearing and impressionable souls of children.

Today there are twenty-six in our family: four married children, three married grandchildren, ten grandchildren and two great-grandchildren. Altogether we have 161 years of marriage in our nuclear family, all with their original spouses! We gather as a family six times each year, and prayer together as a family remains a central part of each gathering. At the lake we even have family worship services with all twenty-six members participating.

Thank You, God, for the divine institution of marriage and family life! Amen.

Roots and Wings

Patricia R. Gottschalk

Each of you should look not only to your own interests, but also to the interests of others. (Philippians 2:4)

So often we tell parents to give their kids "roots and wings." It seems to me that's good advice for newlyweds as well.

We had been married a little over a year when I said to my husband, "Gee, your sister is such a talented artist. I wish I could paint like that." I had never painted; in fact, my elementary art teacher had assured me I had no talent in that direction.

The next day my husband came home with a small Grumbacher oil painting set, a good instruction book and many words of encouragement. "Who said you can't paint as well as my sister, or even better? Give it a try."

Forty years later, when I wanted to take a short-term mission trip to China, lots of people thought I was too old. Not my husband. "Go for it," he said and helped to fund my trip.

I'm still not an artist, and I'm not planning a ministry in China, but the memory of my first attempt at oil painting and the photos of my China trip give me courage to move forward into new adventures. My husband's love and support bind me to him and at the same time set me free to discover who I am.

*Lord, give me eyes to see and a heart to feel the developing passions in my part-
ner's life. Give me strength to help and wisdom to know when to let go. Amen.*

PART TWO

For Better or Worse

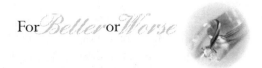

Working on Love

Tracie Peterson

Whatever you do, work at it with all your heart, as working for the Lord, not for men. (Colossians 3:23)

If there's one thing that is an absolute truth, it's this: Marriage is work. It's very hard work.

I married with certain expectations and ideals. Now, after nearly twenty-two years of marriage, I have seen those expectations and ideals go by the wayside to be replaced with something vastly different and infinitely better.

When we married, our pastor reminded us both that not only were we making a commitment to each other; we were also making a commitment to God. He quoted us verses that said it would be better not to make a pledge at all than to make one and not go through with what we'd pledged. Our pastor reminded us that we were not only making a legal agreement but a spiritual contract as well. We no longer had the right to simply call it quits—to get a divorce and dissolve the contract. We had a three-way contractual agreement with God at the head, overseeing it all.

Through the years, that commitment—not to each other, but to God—has kept me from divorcing. There have been moments of sheer frustration and even a few times of great despair, but when I considered my contract, my promise to God, I knew I had to back away from emotions and circumstances and remember that I was working as for the Lord, not for men. Or in this case, for a man—my husband. That thought has taken me from better to worse and back again.

When you find it impossible to work on your marriage for the sake of your husband or even yourself, remember the third partner in this arrangement and work for Him. The benefits are out of this world.

> *Lord, keep my mind, my thoughts and my heart ever on You. Let me seek Your face and remember that the love You have for me and for my husband is infinitely better than anything we can have for one another. In Jesus' name, Amen.*

Celebration—Through Good Times and Bad

Betsy Howard

Trust in the LORD with all your heart and lean not on your own understanding; in all your ways acknowledge him, and he will make your paths straight. (Proverbs 3:5-6)

Rice rained down on us as Will and I ran happily from the church that hot July night more than thirty-three years ago. Just a few minutes before, our families and friends had shared in the solemn celebration of our marriage. They smiled; they cried. They rejoiced with us and prayed for our future together.

From that joyous beginning our life as one unfolded, with celebrations of one kind or another interspersed over the years. Our first Christmas together was filled with love and wonder. A week later, we celebrated my mother's life and said our sad, unexpected good-byes. Six months later our first child, Cathy, arrived. We rejoiced. We thanked God. We celebrated. Two other little girls, Judy and Beth, followed.

Will and I were so happy. We had each other and we had the children we'd always yearned for. Our home resonated with the sounds of children—our own children as well as their playmates. All too soon, car seats and diaper bags were traded for book bags and lunch boxes, and we began to trek back and forth to school to pick up the girls from practice or to cheer them on the hockey field or basketball court. The years flew by, and before we knew it we were dropping Cathy off at college. We cried, but we celebrated too. We were blessed!

Then everything changed. Beth, an eighth grader, no longer wanted to go to school. Confronted by a group of unkind girls during a lunch period, she was consumed with fear. Our happy home became a battleground. Chaos reigned as Beth continued to vacillate between rebelliousness and utter panic. Will and I watched in disbelief as our daughter fell apart. We stood together, taking strength from one another, but without a clue how to help. We began the search for answers—first from our church, then from outside counselors and finally from psychiatrists. Two periods of hospitalization followed. Medications were tried, changed, combined. Our daughter suffered greatly, and Will and I were unable to make things better.

Eventually the doctors agreed upon a diagnosis. "Schizophrenia," they said. "Severe."

"Lord," we cried, "how can this be?"

"Trust Me," He said. "Trust Me."

That was thirteen years ago. Our daughter still suffers daily. She's not been able to hold a job, study for a career or have a boyfriend. She goes to a day program several times a week. She shares her faith with other clients. She tells them that one day she'll be healed. She tells them how much Jesus loves them. She blesses me with help around the house, then walks to the library, the Laundromat and other shops in our little town and leaves copies of the salvation prayer there.

And Will and I wait. We trust our Lord. We stand together as one. And we celebrate our precious daughter. We celebrate the light she brings, even in the darkness. And with her, we celebrate our God.

We thank You, Lord, for the power to celebrate together regardless of the circumstances in our lives. Give us the faith to continue to hope for, and expect, the miracles You have for us. Let us trust that You are in control and that Your timing is perfect. We pray in Jesus' name, Amen.

A Bumpy Wedding Band

Patricia R. Gottschalk

O Israel, put your hope in the LORD, for with the LORD is unfailing love. (Psalm 130:7)

The minister held the small gold ring high so everyone could see. "This ring is a symbol of God's eternal love. Like God's love, this ring has no beginning and no end; it is a perfect circle."

A perfect circle. My mind echoed the words. I looked at my own wedding band and rubbed the inside of it with my thumb. *Well, my wedding band is no longer a perfect circle*, I thought. Actually the present shape of my ring defies description. Maybe *bumpy* would be the right word. Bumpy, as life itself has been sometimes during my marriage. There have been days when the whole world seemed bent out of shape, when tears distorted what I saw, when anger warped my vision.

No one had promised that the wedding ring would keep its perfect shape or that the ring itself was the key to a perfect life. The minister had compared the wedding ring to God's love. During the years, God's perfect love has sustained and strengthened our marriage. His presence with us has kept our marriage "in shape" and our love for each other growing.

Things in life do get bent out of shape—tempers, emotions, finances, even wedding bands. But God's faithful love for us never changes.

Thank You, Lord, that as marriage partners we can count on Your unfailing love to strengthen us and give us wisdom and grace to live with and for each other. Amen.

Marriage Moments

God can paint rich hues on
　　the misty memories of our past.
He can shine a guiding ray
　　on the choices for our future.
But God's love blended with ours
　　reigns best when He, in nearness,
holds this very moment in His hands.

— Charlotte Adelsperger

The Decision to Love

Ann Thorne

A man's heart plans his way, but the LORD directs his steps. (Proverbs 16:9, NKJV)

"She says she doesn't love me anymore," my husband stammered. Each word felt like a grievous blow driving us further into our separate corners. We hung our heads in grief and shame.

We'd married young and committed our marriage to Christ. I'd completed college while my husband went on to finish medical school and an internship. Just when we were making plans for our future, he was drafted and sent to Vietnam as a flight surgeon. I remained stateside with our three young children.

During those years we incurred heavy financial debts, and I had to work full-time. Our relationship grew distant and cold, and the vows we'd made "for better or for worse" now seemed meaningless. The only answer I could envision was to end our marriage and begin life again. I no longer knew my husband. He had returned from Vietnam a different man, and I, in his absence, had become a different woman.

Our counselor grew still and then responded, "In my experience, love is not always based on a feeling. It's at times a decision—a choice. Perhaps if you take some time to know each other again, you can rediscover what you have lost."

Thus began a slow process of healing in our lives. We began to fan that spark with prayer and kindness. Love did return in time. In fact, it had never really left. It just needed to be decided upon and nurtured.

Lord, help me to base my actions on Your Word and the commitments I've made to You and those I love rather than on my feelings. Amen.

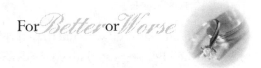

Summer Storm Passing

Debbie Brockett

I would have despaired unless I had believed that I would see the goodness of the LORD in the land of the living. Wait for the LORD; be strong and let your heart take courage; yes, wait for the LORD. (Psalm 27:13-14, NASB)

Leaves rustled down upon the grass as a blustery wind nearly folded the globe willow that shaded our front yard in half. Holding hands and swinging slowly, my husband, Ben, and I were somewhat sheltered from the elements by the deep porch. Off to the south, flashes of lightening, followed by rumbling thunder, rolled across the slate sky. Fascinated, we waited for the summer storm to pass.

I shivered, more from thinking about recent family troubles than from the coolness.

Ben slipped his arm around my shoulders and said, "You all right?"

I nodded and snuggled closer to his side. "Love you."

"Love you too, hon."

Rain began to spatter at our feet, while icy moisture stung our faces. Tucking his feet under the swing, Ben said, "Not going to be a mild one this time."

"They rarely are, dear." I wasn't talking about nature's storms, either.

Within moments it hit with uncharacteristic ferocity. I shook my head when Ben suggested we go inside. Somehow the fierceness of the storm drew my hidden anger and frustration to the surface and carried them away in the drenching swirl.

As quickly as it came, the storm diminished. The rain dripped like diamonds off the willow's leaves and a patch of blue emerged on the horizon. My spirit felt as cleansed as the freshly washed air.

I leaned my head against Ben's shoulder. No matter what storm needed weathering, he was always by my side.

"Seems the storm's passed," Ben noted.

"They always do, dear. Love you."

"Love you too, hon."

Dear Lord, help me to look beyond life's terrible trials and embrace the breathtaking knowledge that You will never leave or forsake me, especially when life is at its hardest. Remind me, especially when my marriage and family are in turmoil, that You have a plan. Amen.

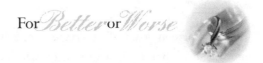

Raspberries and Relationships

Bonnie Doran

Starting a quarrel is like breaching a dam; so drop the matter before a dispute breaks out. (Proverbs 17:14)

It was the raspberries.

John and I had been married for just a few weeks. He was helping me carry groceries to the kitchen when he spied a box of raspberries in one of the sacks. He immediately ripped off the plastic cover and started devouring them.

Steam wafted out of my ears. "Don't eat those raspberries! They haven't been washed!" He mumbled something (with his mouth full) and kept eating.

Thus began the first argument to mar our marital bliss. Like most arguments, it started with something insignificant and ended up revealing a deeper problem.

John was hurt. I was yelling at him for eating raspberries! He wasn't going to get sick because a little dirt was left on them. Why was I so upset?

The real issue wasn't that the raspberries were dirty but that John stopped helping me. I felt he was paying more attention to those berries than to my needs. But because I couldn't recognize what I felt and verbalize it, the raspberries became the focal point of our quarrel rather than the underlying problem. It took a few strained vocal cords and tears before we got to the root of the conflict.

After thirteen years of marriage, I'm a little better at arguments. Now when I get steamed, I try to look at the real issue, not the raspberries. Sometimes it's best to keep my mouth shut, especially if I'm cranky or the issue is minor. At other times, it's best to tell John what I'm feeling and why. Most of the time, we deal with the real issue, not the one on the surface. That makes us both happy.

After all, raspberries are better fresh than steamed.

Lord, conflicts are inevitable when two sinful human beings live together. Help us stop the arguments before they start and deal with the real issues, not the raspberries. Amen.

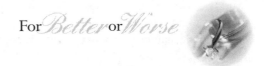

"You Never Said Anything About That!"

Clint Kelly

But may the righteous be glad and rejoice before God; may they be happy and joyful. (Psalm 68:3)

As soon as the announcer said, "Win an all-expense-paid trip for two to the Rose Bowl!" I was all over that radio contest.

Christmas was coming, and here was the perfect surprise for my wife—the Rose Parade, sunny California for New Year's and best of all, we'd get to visit our daughter and son-in-law who lived there. It wouldn't cost us a cent. What joy this would bring my beloved!

That I would get to watch my prized University of Washington Huskies football team take on Purdue at the Rose Bowl live had, of course, nothing to do with my excitement. Well, almost nothing.

"All you have to do is tell us what you would be willing to do on the radio to win this trip, then do it!" Hmmm. What would I do?

My wife held her breath.

It was worse than she expected.

Soon after, on a Friday morning during the 7-8 o'clock rush hour, I went on the air and devoured a bowl of Milk-bone dog biscuits in milk—eighteen biscuits in a variety of flavors, including beef and turkey. I would have been fine but for the helpful caller who explained just what "chicken byproducts" in the ingredients actually meant.

Never mind. California was great. The Huskies won. Our daughter and her husband were a delight.

Did I mention it didn't cost us a cent?

But as much as she enjoyed herself on that trip, my wife had agreed to marry a writer, not a radio stunt man. Our wedding vows did not include "I take thee . . . in wackiness and stability. . . ." Thousands of listeners heard me crunch and slurp my breakfast of dog biscuits. Was going public like that fair to my dear, low-profile wife?

Sure. Most of the time we are the typical "people next door." We mow our lawn, pay our taxes and buy toothpaste in the economy size. But every once in a while it is great fun to do the unexpected. Marriage benefits from a pleasant twist now and then. A catered meal. A singing telegram. A surprise trip earned in a way they're still talking about down at the old water cooler.

Avoid boring predictability and you too might hear those sweet, reassuring words, "You did *what?!*"

Kind Father, keep me from becoming a boring mate. Thank You for the joy of being alive in Christ. Teach me to spread that joy to my wife by showing her how much creativity she sparks in me. Amen.

Forgiveness Matters

Dawn Janho

If you hold anything against anyone, forgive him, so that your Father in heaven may forgive you your sins. (Mark 11:25)

At age twenty-four Tim and I had been married for five years. He made several poor decisions during those years, and now we faced losing everything.

Tim prepared himself for my words.

"I feel shame and anger," I quietly spoke through my tears. "I wanted to leave you because I'm tired of forgiving you. Yet I chose to stay because I know this is what Christ wants of me. In spite of everything, your love toward me has left an impact on my life. You hurt me deeply, but there is a part of me that still believes in you. My hope is that you will fulfill your promises and change. I want you to become the spiritual leader of our family."

Tim hugged me and softly said, "I promise you, I will change...."

One year went by, and the changes I had longed for did not occur.

I went to Tim in a final attempt to save our marriage. "Do you remember when you initiated the idea of attending the Word of Life Bible Institute? My support still remains should you choose to go. In order to be with you, I am willing to move our family out of the state, but Tim, your willingness to say 'yes' to Christ must come first. Your decision will show me what direction our marriage will take."

I left the house.

When I came back home, Tim met me at the door with tears in his eyes and a smile on his face. "Honey, when you left, I took out my Bible and knelt down to pray. I had a heart-to-heart talk with the Lord, and I made the decision to attend the Institute."

Moved by his news and filled with new hope, I trembled as I embraced him.

At the Institute, our first student assembly took place around a bonfire. The speaker extended an invitation to come forward in order to rededicate our lives to Christ. Tim took his first step in spiritual leadership as he reached for my hand and led us forward. We were given sticks that represented our past. Privately we asked Christ to forgive us, and then we asked His future blessing on our marriage. As we cried and held one another, we threw the sticks into the blazing fire and watched our sins burn away.

Our marriage did survive as Christ became the true source of healing and strength in our lives. He brought us peace and harmony.

To this day, I still thank Christ for whispering in my ear that forgiveness matters.

Lord, at times my heart is wounded and I don't feel like being pleasant or forgiving. I ask for Your help in remaining respectful to my partner as I choose to walk in obedience and to forgive freely. Amen.

Let It Snow!

Brenda Nixon

It is hard to stop a quarrel once it starts, so don't let it begin. (Proverbs 17:14, TLB)

"We'll never make it!" my husband, Paul, insisted.

"Yes, we will!" I maintained.

"It's too snowy."

"No, it's not."

We wanted to attend church one wintry Sunday when we were still newlyweds. I grew up in the Snow Belt and felt confident about plowing through near-blizzard conditions. With a last look out the window, Paul conceded, "If you drive, we'll try getting to church." We did.

Snow accumulated during the service. Afterward we quickly bid good-bye to the meager group of "die hards." I climbed in the driver's seat as Paul settled his seatbelt. As snow crunched beneath our tires, we eased onto an abandoned street. "This isn't bad," I declared.

"We're not home yet!" Paul countered.

Turning a corner near home, we slid into a curb and halted. I stepped on the accelerator and said, "We'll get out." The tires spun, rolled forward and settled back into a furrow. I shifted; we rolled slightly back only to hear the squeal of sliding rubber.

Paul smugly announced, "We're stuck." We sat momentarily, our breath steaming the windows. Without a sound he threw open the door and trudged to the rear of our car. "Gun it when I say!" he hollered. The squeal of sliding rubber echoed through the air as Paul pushed against the bumper. Repeatedly we struggled to dislodge our car.

"Where ya going?" I asked, watching him tromp through knee-high snow toward our apartment.

"To get a shovel!" he retorted.

Paul returned, a shovel slung over his shoulder. Hoisting piles of snow from around the tires, he occasionally peered at me over his fogged glasses. At his urge, I again pressed the pedal and our car jerked forward. He jumped in and growled, "Let's go!" As we inched down the street to our driveway, Paul moaned, "We shouldn't have gone."

"So what?" I justified. "We're home now." Privately I thought, *He doesn't have to get mad about this.* Then God reminded me that Paul had grown up where snow merely dusted the ground. I pictured those times to look like a brownie sprinkled with confectioner's sugar. Paul considered this season a nuisance. I was challenged by it. Who was right or wrong or in charge wasn't the issue. We were a union of two people with two different perceptions. Our differences should never escalate into a division.

Times of agreement and disagreement are my "better or worse" in marriage. They serve as my opportunity to learn about my partner and to practice the generous nature of God.

Leaning over, I whispered, "I'm sorry I didn't respect your hesitation about going out in this."

"Sorry I got upset," he replied. "I understand you more, and someday we'll laugh at this."

Today we do!

Father, help us to accommodate each other. Only through Your grace can we come together. Through Your example of forgiveness we can continue to live and learn together. Make our marriage a union, not a contest. Amen.

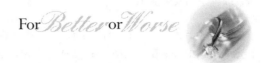

Ol' Blue Eyes

Susan Reith Swan

A man finds joy in giving an apt reply—and how good is a timely word! (Proverbs 15:23)

The natural light of the wintry day glowed on Tom's face. *He has the most beautiful blue eyes I've ever seen,* I thought as I listened to him talk, drinking in the exquisite color. *Should I tell him?*

I couldn't remember the last time I had studied my husband of thirteen years so closely. Lately we hadn't paid much attention to each other except to complain, nag or criticize. A few days earlier I had even contemplated the feasibility of moving the kids and me in with my parents. Five months of Tom's unemployment were taking their toll.

I focused my attention back to his detailed account of breakfast with an acquaintance from church. This man had generously offered his time to go over Tom's résumé and give him some job search pointers. The more Tom talked, the more confidence returned to his voice and manner.

He turned and walked to the hall. *Thank You, Lord,* I thought as I followed him. *You knew how much Tom needed those encouraging words.*

"You know what I noticed while you were standing by the window?" I asked.

He cocked his head, wrinkled his eyebrows, then broke into a smile. "My mustache," he replied.

"Well, that too," I stammered, surprised he remembered how much I love his mustache. "But that's not what I meant." I described how the light had intensified the beauty of his eyes. He concentrated on me, then pulled me close.

"We need to hug more," he said. "There hasn't been much tenderness around here lately."

"Why don't I call Mom to babysit tonight so we can use that two-for-one dinner coupon?"

"Good idea," he said.

What a difference a caring friend and a compliment make, I thought on my way to the phone, looking forward to spending the whole evening studying those eyes.

> *Lord, help me to remember the pricelessness of caring words and loving thoughts. When I am tempted to focus on the negative, remind me how much love is found in the simple things. Amen.*

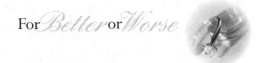

Memory Quilting

Linda Evans Shepherd

Everyone born of God overcomes the world. (1 John 5:4)

One evening my husband and I sat in an open-air restaurant. Paul asked, "Would you have married me if you had known that our only daughter would be so severely disabled?"

I felt the night breeze rearrange my curls as I thought through the events of our recent past. I thought of the ten months Laura had spent in a coma, of all the emotional suffering that had stitched itself into a shroud of grief. I thought of Laura's recently acquired wheelchair and life-support systems. "No," I finally whispered, willing to throw away the past in exchange for relief from my pain.

Paul stared at his grilled snapper, unable to look at me.

"I'm sorry," I said. "I love you, but I would have done anything to have prevented Laura from being hurt, even if that meant never meeting you."

Later I rummaged through the remains of a friend's household goods. "Take anything you want," Vicki said. "I'm throwing out these things because they remind me of my soon-to-be-ex-husband. I have a new love now, and I don't want these things to remind me of the past."

As I looked at the remains of Vicki's discarded memories, I changed my mind about my answer to Paul's question. My memories, even those which were painful, were now precious to me.

Other memories began playing through my mind like bright ribbons of color—the early marriage water fights we'd splashed through our lime-green apartment . . . the day Paul had almost squeezed off my fingers as I birthed our son . . . how hard Paul had worked to build our cedar fence so baby Laura and then Jimmy could toddle about the backyard of our first home.

Yes, some of our memories were dark. But as I evaluated them I realized how even they enriched the quilted pattern they helped to create.

Later that night, I reached for Paul's hand as we sat together on the sofa. "I'm sorry I told you I wouldn't have married you if I had known our daughter would one day be severely disabled."

Paul's blue eyes met mine.

I squeezed his hand. "I'm glad I married you. Despite what we've been through, we've been through it together, and I wouldn't change that for anything."

Paul wrapped his arm around my shoulders. "I feel the same way."

I snuggled closer to my husband, glad I had someone committed to making the heirloom memories with me as long as the Lord would allow. And with things in fresher perspective, I was going to make sure I cherished every patchwork moment of the crazy-quilt that had become our lives.

Dear Lord, life's journey may have many twists and turns. Help my spouse and me never to be divided by turning away from each other or by turning away from You. Help us to travel the right path together. Thank You for giving us one another, and thank You for making the journey with us, every step of the way. Amen.

[From *Faith Never Shrinks in Hot Water: Inspirational Stories for Women Who Want Their Faith to Grow*, © 1996 Linda E. Shepherd. Published by Pacific Press Publishing Association.]

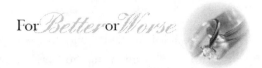

Peace in the Midst

Alexandra Scott

Don't worry about anything; instead, pray about everything. Tell God what you need, and thank him for all he has done. If you do this, you will experience God's peace, which is far more wonderful than the human mind can understand. His peace will guard your hearts and minds as you live in Christ Jesus. (Philippians 4:6-7, NLT)

When I gave my heart to the Lord four years ago, nothing prepared me for the great joys I would experience in Christ and the many sorrows I would encounter in my marriage.

Overnight I became a woman who attended church regularly, read her Bible daily and entered into an intimate, dynamic relationship with her Lord. Overnight a spiritual tug-of-war broke out between my husband and me that rocked the very foundation of our marriage.

"Why do you have to go to church on Sundays? Why do you have to read your Bible every day? And why must you pray?" he asked grudgingly. He wanted the "old me" back—desperately. He wanted the woman who sipped coffee and chatted with him on Sunday mornings instead of going to church.

The more I talked about Jesus, the more he cringed. The more I pressured him to go to church, the farther we grew apart. I felt frustration, anger, fear, loneliness and—at times—deep despair. So did my husband. I worried about our marriage breaking up. I felt guilty that I wasn't winning him to Christ. I found no peace.

But as I persisted in prayer, God renewed my hope and my strength to live out the marriage vows "for better or for worse." He helped me to stop worrying and to trust Him fully. Even though my husband hasn't embraced Christ as Savior, he attends church regularly and has become more attentive, loving and kind.

God assures me that it's not my fault my husband isn't a Christian, and that He isn't withholding my blessing. After all, "he who did not spare his own Son, but gave him up for us all—how will he not also, along with him, graciously give us all things?" (Romans 8:32). God wants my husband to be saved more than I do. But it will be His Holy Spirit that draws him. Nothing else (Zechariah 4:6).

I'm now able to thank the Lord, praise Him and worship Him in all circumstances. And what He promised has finally come true. His peace has overtaken me. I'm now at rest.

Lord, please encourage me to talk to You about everything so I don't worry and lose hope. Give me Your wisdom and strength to get through the dark times, and let Your peace reign in my heart. Amen.

For *Better* or *Worse*

A Stronger Bond
Through Trials

Milton and Merilyn Fisher

Because Your unfailing love is better than life, my lips praise You.
(Psalm 63:3, author's translation)

Twelve years in Ethiopia together gave us problems enough, but nothing life-threatening or marriage-shaking. A previous two-year pastorate and six years of interspersed graduate studies were weathered smoothly. Three children brought the usual parental responsibilities and occasional difficulties, complicated at times by travels and by life abroad.

The years rolled along, and the grand adventure continued. Spread out over twenty-two years of teaching for Dad and part-time geriatric nursing for Mom were some dozen more trips abroad. Some of those involved extended assignments in Bible translation work (the New International Version) and archaeological excavations in Israel. These too were mostly "fun," and we continued to thank our Lord that there were only minor problems with our growing youngsters and that all three were eager to follow the Savior. With God's kind providence and blessing, life grew increasingly better. It seemed so easy to serve Him.

Suddenly the scene changed—a flood of trouble. The year was 1990. So much happened at once those first four months.

Clearing out our big old house and squeezing into a much smaller one was painful. Milt started the year with an internal infection, son Marty slipped on ice and broke his ankle and his brother Mike's wife spent some time in the hospital. We did our best to assist both families. Month two brought an operation for a malignancy for Mom DeMott and a disturbing family problem for daughter Marjorie down in Texas. House repairs continued through March, despite a full-time teaching load. Then in early April Mike underwent eye repair for a detached retina. More grandchild care. Also in April we spent two weeks on mission business in France and Tunisia. Final work on the house left just forty-five minutes to pack for the overseas flight!

That quarter-year was the most stressful we'd gone through together. But God gave us wings (Isaiah 40:31). The worst, however, was yet to come. In mid-October, 1992, our firstborn son Marty was diagnosed as having a malignant brain tumor. Despite surgery plus X-ray- and chemotherapy, his condition was terminal. It was his fortieth year, our forty-second of marriage. Our heavenly Father gave Marty grace, patience and true nobility. He never cried, never asked, "Why?" That helped so much. During nine months of loving but stressful caregiving, our wonderful Savior continued to strengthen our marriage through trial. He taught us to pray with deeper understanding, "Your eyes saw me yet unborn, and upon Your book were written every one of my allotted days, before any of them existed" (Psalm 139:16, author's translation).

Thank You, Lord, for this assurance from Your Word. None of the emergencies or afflictions of our lives need shake our faith or threaten our marriage bond in Christ. May we ever find strength in the power of Your unfailing love. In Jesus' precious name, Amen.

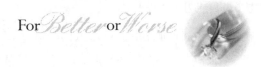

Do Something!

Marjorie Geary Vawter

Not that we are sufficient of ourselves to think any thing as of ourselves; but our sufficiency is of God. (2 Corinthians 3:5, KJV)

This morning our sewer line backed up—again. No, it wasn't a surprise. In the two years we have been in this house, we have been "blessed" with this problem several times. The most memorable was last Christmas when we had a house full of people and we couldn't even flush the toilet!

I was doing laundry preparatory to leaving the country on a mission trip with my husband when the sewer backed up the first time. As soon as I surveyed the stinky mess on my basement floor, I called the one person I was sure had the answer to the problem—my husband.

When it comes to plumbing, Roger has more experience and knowledge than the average do-it-yourselfer, so the sewer line backing up shouldn't have been above his capabilities.

He tried several "can't fail" remedies—but they all failed. Meanwhile, my frustration level was reaching the boiling point.

"Why didn't that work?"

"Why can't you fix it?"

"I need it fixed now, not next week!"

"Can you call somebody?" (I temporarily forgot that statement meant he would have to admit defeat in something he had some expertise in.)

Finally I used the ultimate threat. "You are not meeting the needs I have to live in a secure environment. Do something, and do it now!"

The night before we were to leave for Ecuador, Roger admitted defeat and called a twenty-four-hour plumbing service to come out and unclog the line—only to have it happen again when we returned.

I'm a slow learner, but I finally caught on to the fact that the Lord had something for me to learn from a broken sewer line. Husbands are not capable of meeting every need their wives have. Only God is sufficient to meet every need.

Oh, I still call on Roger when the sewer line backs up. Most of the time I let him know that I'm not expecting him to do anything. And now he calls the plumber.

> *Father, our sufficiency is in You. Remind me that only You can meet all my needs. Help me to learn to rely on You for all I need and to praise You. Amen.*

For *Better* or *Worse*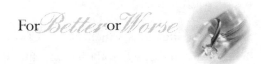

Socks and Other Little Things

Anita L. Fordyce

The heart of her husband doth safely trust in her, so that he shall have no need of spoil. (Proverbs 31:11, KJV)

We had been married less than six months when he came to me and held out six socks with no mates. He didn't find it funny when I quipped, "Into the washer his socks went in pairs—like magic abracadabra—they came out in spares." He didn't understand that I hadn't intended to lose one-half of six pairs of his socks. He never lost anything, or so it seemed; everything he owned had a particular place. My things were everywhere—mostly in piles. He was totally frustrated with me and was taking this sock thing very personally.

I didn't think my marriage would end over socks, but before it got worse, I prayed for help. God didn't help me find the socks, but He showed me a way to keep them all together. I found a wonderful nylon bag with a zipper. I presented it to my new groom as a solution. We agreed that he would put his pairs of socks in the bag; I would zip it shut and throw them in the wash. When I put his socks into the wash—no magic abracadabra—they came out in pairs. That was twenty-nine years ago, and we've not lost a sock since.

Learning to live with a neat man and caring about his needs was the greater challenge. He felt he couldn't trust me to care for what seemed to me to be little things but which were big to him. It was important to remove the causes of the distrust—to avoid and change situations which allowed frustration. With God's help, I learned that when these little things were cared for, my husband and I could face bigger challenges together.

Father, thank You for a husband who taught me that little things matter. Help me to see and take care of those little things today. Amen.

Whispers in the Garden

Joy R. Jacobs

Do not grieve the Holy Spirit of God. . . . Get rid of all bitterness, rage and anger. (Ephesians 4:30-31)

My father had been overprotective and jealous; at the age of nineteen, I married a man who was just the opposite. The ministry in which my husband was involved took him away from me often, sometimes for long stretches of time—and he seemed to enjoy every minute of it! And I, who had longed for freedom in my teenage years, found that my new freedom left me feeling—again—terribly insecure.

For the first three years of our marriage I was able to travel with my husband on occasion, but then life changed drastically with two "blessed events." I gave birth to two active, healthy little boys within fourteen months of each other.

Gradually, my insecurity bred anxiety and resentment. Like Ancestress Eve, I listened to the serpent, who whispered: "Can it really be that God has called only your husband into ministry? Are you not also intelligent? Do you not have a college degree? Look how mundane *your* work is compared to his. While he travels and sings and meets new people, does God expect you to be content with bottles and diapers—and bills?"

And like Eve, Eve's daughter began to ponder these things. And she ate of the tree of resentment and the root of bitterness, whose seed had been sown in earlier years, took hold and began to grow. And her garden became a wilderness dominated by thorns and thistles.

It was easy to start feeling sorry for myself again, to slip back into familiar patterns of negative reactions. After all, no one was concerned about *my* personal needs.

God has unique ways of dealing with each of us. This great and glorious Elohim-Jehovah, in addition to His creative imagination, has a wonderful sense of humor.

Remember Miriam, the "I-am-Miriam-I-am-right" sister of Moses and Aaron, who found her critical spirit and bitterness chastened by the dreaded disease of leprosy? Well, Miriam and I will reminisce together in heaven! At the age of twenty-nine I was struck down with the undignified curse of chicken pox. For three weeks I was deathly sick, so helplessly sick I could hardly get from my bedroom to the bathroom, much less take care of my not-as-sick children.

God's sense of humor? His perfect timing? Only one reason has ever kept my itinerant husband at home in bed for more than a day or two, and that is a recurring back problem. Sure enough, those back muscles collapsed during the second week I was confined to bed.

Bob was in so much pain that he couldn't move. I was pathetically weak and ugly with scabs literally covering my face and scalp. We couldn't walk away from each other, as we had been doing for so long. We were forced to talk to each other—for a whole week!

We talked. We cried. We began to penetrate more than surface issues. We recognized wrongs. We confessed to each other. We confessed to the Lord. We forgave. He forgave. The God of righteousness and holiness was at work. The God of love was healing our marriage.

Thank You, Jehovah-rapha, for the times in our marriage when Your chastening was a prerequisite to healing. Amen.

[From *When God Seems Far Away*, © 1988 Joy Jacobs. Published by Tyndale House Publishers, 1988; Christian Publications, 2000.]

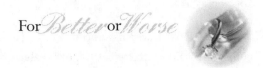

"Get a Grip!"
Judith Howard

Do not be anxious about anything, but in everything, by prayer and petition, with thanksgiving, present your requests to God. And the peace of God, which transcends all understanding, will guard your hearts and your minds in Christ Jesus. (Philippians 4:6–7)

I can be fretful. It was transmitted to me in the genetic squiggles I inherited from my mother, a world-class worrier.

When we lived in Hawaii, my husband frequently took three-week business trips to the Orient. After such a junket, a gate mix-up had my young son and me waiting, and waiting, and waiting for him at the airport.

"Please page my missing husband!" I tearfully pleaded. "Is there a place to report him missing?" I darted around seeking help—somewhere, anywhere!

When we were reunited hours later, my husband's strong, consoling arms sheltered me, even as he offered good-natured, if firmly stated, advice: "Get a grip!"

Many years have passed. I have made progress in overcoming my faith lapses, even though they have not been completely licked. Needless to say, when my trust lags, there have been some interesting discussions in our home. "You've taught. . . .Why not. . . ." You get the idea.

The Bible is clear. I have no recourse. No matter what the circumstances, no matter what might be ahead—good, bad or routine—Paul tells us, "Do not be anxious about *anything*" (Philippians 4:6).

In those fearful, fretful moments when I'm convinced I've been widowed or rendered childless, when I'm sure the Lord has turned His back, I'm to trust Him. And that's just the beginning—I'm to *give thanks* in the clinches as I make my requests!

Loving and patient Lord, help me to trust You. I determine now, before the next stress pushes me to waver, that I will depend on You. Leaning on You, may I give thanks in the midst of trials and suffering, offering my husband more of the better and less of the worse. Amen.

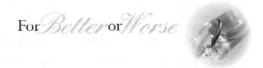

The Power of Three

Kate Paffett

And now just as you trusted Christ to save you, trust him, too, for each day's problems; live in vital union with him. Let your roots grow down into him and draw up nourishment from him. See that you go on growing in the Lord, and become strong and vigorous in the truth you were taught. Let your lives overflow with joy and thanksgiving for all he has done. (Colossians 2:6-7, TLB)

Although twenty-five years have passed, one moment from my wedding stands out as clearly as if it happened yesterday—walking hand-in-hand with my father, putting one foot in front of the other, praying, "Lord, I hope the love I feel today will be enough to make this last forever."

Bill and I marvel when we think about how young we were back then. We truly grew up together in those first several years of married life.

Growing up can bring with it the opportunity of growing closer together or the disadvantage of growing far apart. We have had great joys, but we have also endured trials. During the times when we felt our paths were separating, I often asked the Lord to help us find our way back to one another. The Lord answered my prayers; only at the time, I didn't know it.

We suffered many losses: loss of jobs, loss of parents, loss of children. And when we allowed the busyness of life to intrude, we almost lost each other. Navigating through the murky waters of uncertainty seemed futile at times. But we prevailed through each suffering. When my mother died, Bill was my rock. When he lost his job, I was his. Even when we buried babies, we leaned on one another.

It would have been easy to leave during the dark times. But something held us there. Had we walked out, we never would have come to know all we could have been. It took some time before I realized it, but that is how the Lord answered my prayers. Throughout all the uncertainty, one thing remained constant. You see, three people stood on that altar as we exchanged vows—Bill, me and God. And it's been the three of us ever since.

Today I walk hand-in-hand with my husband, placing one foot in front of the other. That new, young love that I thought was so powerful all those years ago was merely a springboard from which this older, wiser love now exists and continues to grow, a love that has been transformed because of the hardships it has weathered and the prayers that never ceased.

Lord, in good times may we praise You. In bad times remind us to turn to You. Amen.

Kidnapped!

Verda J. Glick

God is our refuge and strength, a very present help in trouble. (Psalm 46:1, KJV)

I knew something was wrong that night when I heard my oldest son's pickup in our driveway. Taking me in his arms, Ernest told me, "Mama, robbers kept Papa on the mountain. They're asking for ransom. Come, sit down."

My husband, Eli, had gone as usual to hold a weekly preaching service at El Paste, a mountain in western El Salvador. Ernest explained that bandits had captured Eli and the twenty-four persons who had gone with him. When the kidnappers released the group, they had told the driver, "We will keep the pastor. Tell his wife to send us $11,500. His oldest son must deliver the ransom alone. If he's not here with the money by 2 o'clock tomorrow afternoon, we'll kill our captive."

My knees felt weak and tightness constricted my chest. "Oh, son," I stammered, "let's pray." We fell on our knees by the old brown sofa and asked God for wisdom to know what to do.

For the first time, our roles reversed. Ernest was strong; I was weak. He cared for me; I depended on him. I wept on his chest; he wrapped his arms around me and reassured me.

How could I let my son go up that mountain to deliver the ransom? I needed him. He possessed maturity I had never seen in him before. I wanted him to stay with me.

My love for my husband made me want to pay the ransom as quickly as possible. My love for my son made me want to hold him back. I felt torn between my love for both of them.

After an agony of indecision, I knew I must send Ernest to deliver the ransom. After weeping in his arms once more and kissing him good-bye, I let him carry the big package of money to the pickup and drive away. With a troubled heart, I turned to the One who sent His only Son to deliver the ransom for me.

My heavenly Father, who didn't spare His own Son from that dangerous mission, now filled me with strength and peace while my son went on his. Hours later, both my husband and son returned home safely.

I have a deeper appreciation now for the love that compelled God to send His Son to deliver the ransom for me. That love sustained me in one of the most difficult situations I have ever faced.

Thank You, Father God, for sending Your Son to deliver the ransom for me. You are my help in times of trouble, my refuge and strength. I thank You for Your care over my loved ones. Amen.

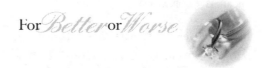

Sanctuary

Laney Scott

This is My commandment, that you love one another as I have loved you. (John 15:12, NKJV)

The woman's words pelted me like icy rain, stinging my skin and freezing my heart. The allegations she was making . . . could they be true? Twenty years ago my husband suggested what? To whom? My head was spinning with confusion and fear. I inhaled betrayal with every bitter breath.

I searched my memory, and later, my journals, to recall the time in our marriage her accusations covered. Yes, even then I was confused. Things seemed strained and strange between my husband and me. My writings reflected vague concern. Something was going on.

Anyone who has experienced love's betrayal can identify with my state. For weeks following the woman's accusations I was disoriented, confused. Was she right? Could this have happened? Would he have done this? Who was this person I was married to? And why am I finding this out now? What am I supposed to do with this bad "old" news?

Mechanically I went through my days: work, shopping, laundry, children, work, shopping, laundry, children. My thoughts were far away, often spinning in circles—circles with razor-sharp edges.

Instinctively I sought God. I read my Bible, prayed and journaled. "Where are You, God?" I asked. "What is the truth? Please help me," I begged. I dug down deep for my spiritual roots.

As I sought God, He began to speak to me through His Word, through a few trusted friends and through prayer. And then His voice rang loud and clear as I listened to a tape of Dr. Henry Blackaby, author of *Experiencing God*: "Will you love your husband with the same quality of love that I have had for you? Will you forgive him with the same quality of forgiveness that I have had for you?"

What had God forgiven me for? How much had He loved me?

Step by step I began walking through the catalog of my failures. Selfishness, anger, pride, unbelief and yes, unfaithfulness, all took their place in the parade of my sins. I thanked Him for forgiving me for each and every sin I could remember. His love for me spilled into my life like Niagara Falls.

Now, could I forgive and love like that? Only with His help. Desperately I clung to God, and slowly He began walking me down the trail of reconciliation and healing, gently leading me, encouraging me and building my faith. Forgiven, I found I could forgive a lot. Loved, I could love deeply and well. God would show me how.

"Love one another as I have loved you." A simple sentence, a profound principle.

> *Father, thank You for the unfathomable depths of Your love and forgiveness. I want to reflect Your character in my world. Teach me, Lord, to walk this walk of faith. Amen.*

Letting Go of the
Victim Mentality

Steffani Powell

For you know that it was not with perishable things such as silver or gold that you were redeemed from the empty way of life handed down to you from your forefathers, but with the precious blood of Christ, a lamb without blemish or defect. (1 Peter 1:18-19)

My husband and I both grew up in alcoholic homes, which may account for the problems we have with trusting and believing the best of each other. When the communication lines are down in our marriage and we're both wounded, God sometimes calls in His own repairmen to help us. Little did I suspect His strategy recently when, in the midst of a crisis, I called my dearest friend, who lives over two hours away.

As I poured out my load of frustrations with our marriage and our finances, Dixie interrupted hesitantly. "Well . . . I say this with fear and trembling, but we've always been able to be honest with each other. I think I hear a sort of 'victim mentality' in your voice, maybe even a whine."

I confess I was speechless for a full thirty seconds. Then I felt a sense of relief.

"It's hard to face, but you're right," I admitted. "I can see I've let myself fall into my old bad habits of blaming and complaining. Not only have I made life miserable for Ned, but I've quit taking care of my own part of the problems," I told her, chagrined but grateful for her honesty.

That phone conversation turned me around. I repented before God. Our problems weren't resolved immediately, but I was freed to take an honest inventory of my own responsibilities and needs. I worked out a household budget that covered the areas for which I was accountable. With my husband's permission I joined a cell group even though he wasn't ready for one.

I let go of resentments. I began to give up the expectations that were at the root of those resentments. I forgave Ned and he forgave me. Then I worked on releasing him to respond to the situations that confronted us in his time and in his way without pressure from me to do it differently. As the load of care rolled off my back into the Lord's hands, I was surprised at how much smaller those same problems looked on this side of the cross.

Dear Father God, no matter how any of us grew up or what lies we've believed along our journeys, You have awesome ways of bringing home the truth that sets us free. Each time You deliver us out of the chaos we've created, we realize anew how very dependent we are on Your love to heal and sustain our relationships. In Jesus we have genuine hope that the destructive, sinful patterns passed down through the generations are being broken for us and for our children. Thank You, Lord. Amen.

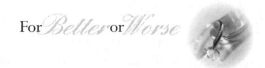

Gathering Pearls

Carol Carolan

There will be showers of blessing. (Ezekiel 34:26)

Marriage can be the best of times . . . and the worst of times. If we trust the Lord and keep a sense of humor, it can be a wonderful ride on life's roller coaster, but gathering pearls on a roller coaster is no easy task. Pearls, you say? Yep, pearls!

If you've ever broken a string of pearls, you know how they go all over the place, bouncing and rolling in every direction. Months later you find them under a table or in a corner, sometimes right in the middle of the room!

God's blessings are like pearls dropped from heaven. They don't stop when times are tough, but it's up to us to watch for them. I keep them in an imaginary black velvet bag and write them in a journal. This way, on a day when I may not see the pearls or think God has forgotten me, I can remember past blessings.

Let me share one of my pearls with you.

My husband is a kind, gentle, quiet man—a peaceful man, slow to anger and even slower to angry action. I love this about him, because I tend to be emotional, and his calm keeps me calm. However, I also want my Prince Charming to "slay" dragons for me, a task which doesn't necessarily go along with his gentle personality.

Recently our daughter spent a semester studying in Samoa and New Zealand. She lived in grass huts, slept on floors and ate who-knows-what. Needless to say, I was very stressed, especially when we got a call in the middle of the night telling us that she and several of the other students had somehow gotten staph infections. It was no surprise to me. After all, she was living in "deplorable" conditions in the middle of nowhere! They probably didn't even have any "real" doctors! (Can you tell I was just a little over the edge?) When I got off the phone, I told my husband he needed to get his passport because we were going to New Zealand. And also he needed to put on his armor, get the horse out of the stable and go slay a dragon—NOW!

John put his arms around me and told me that they do have real doctors in Samoa and that Dawn was on antibiotics. He reminded me that we needed to trust that God was in control. He spent the rest of that day finding a long-distance carrier that also had collect calling codes so our daughter would be able to call any time, from any phone, day or night. He did slay the dragon for me, but in his own calm, dependable and purposeful way. Needless to say, I gathered pearls that day. And, yes, my daughter fully recovered and spent the rest of the semester gathering her own pearls.

Help us, Lord, to keep looking for the pearls on life's roller coaster and to enjoy the ride! Amen.

The Meaning of "Worse"

R.C. Zitzer

Praise be to the God . . . who comforts us in all our troubles, so that we can comfort those in any trouble with the comfort we ourselves have received from God. (2 Corinthians 1:3-4)

When "for better or for worse" is spoken at a wedding ceremony, it is at a time of hope and expectation, a euphoric time when "better" seems assured and "worse" can scarcely be imagined. This was true one mild May morning as I looked into the bluest of blue eyes and said "I do" to my new bride.

"Better" filled the days following our wedding. It kept us company during our honeymoon and was with us in our planning, packing and moving several states away so I could attend college. "Better" was a little apartment that we loved and the news of our first baby on the way.

I liked "better." I was getting used to it.

But "worse" found us quickly. It descended on us one evening with inexplicable pains and uncontrolled bleeding. It followed us to the hospital and became visible in a doctor's furrowed brow and audible as hushed voices in the hall. It sat vigil during a premature birth I was not permitted to attend, displayed itself in the downcast faces of the medical staff and shimmered in the tears of a nurse who took my hand and said, "I'm so sorry."

"Worse" took shape as a document giving the hospital permission to dispose of the tiny body and rode on the bleak December wind that blew against the windows. It relentlessly reminded us of the 1,400 miles that separated us from friends and family and became a rare, deafening silence between us when words would not comfort. It stole the joy from my poor little bride with the blue eyes who had felt the life within her, experienced the doctor visits, the labor pains and the hospital stay, but had no baby to bring home. "Worse" found us awake during the endless nights of that first year, her crying for her baby and my pacing the apartment, unable to help, unable to sleep, unable to find the "better."

Now, twenty years and three healthy children later, I have seen plenty of "better." I've seen that God uses both to solidify a relationship. And I've seen our oldest daughter, now in college, open her heart to Christ because we were able by God's grace to answer her many questions about where her big sister lives. And I praise Him each day for that girl with the bluest of blue eyes to whom I still cling—for better or worse.

Father, help us to see Your hand in all of life, but especially in the relationships that You've ordained. Amen.

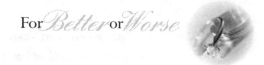

Frozen Faith

Susan Petropulos

Now faith is being sure of what we hope for and certain of what we do not see. (Hebrews 11:1)

"I love you," my husband pleaded through the telephone.

"Uh-huh," was my flat reply.

The separation was in its seventh month and seemed to be headed nowhere. The distance between us was much more than a mere 250 miles.

It had been my decision to put the marriage on hold. I didn't hate my husband, but I didn't love him either. After seventeen years I wanted out. I wasn't sure how it had happened, and I really didn't care. I knew that the marriage had been a mistake and so had trusting God. A loving God would not have let this happen to me!

Week after week I fought off my husband's attempts at reconciliation. Week after week I sought new ways to shake my fist at God. I went out to bars, nightclubs and parties. I tried to pretend I was OK, but inside I knew that this "new life" was not really what I wanted.

But there was something that I didn't know. People were praying. And as they prayed, my life changed. I can't tell you the day or the hour when it happened, but gradually I began to shake my fist at God less and to reach out to Him more. Instead of the trips to bars and nightclubs, I began to attend a church. Exposed to the powerful warmth of Christ's love, my frozen heart slowly came to life again. I decided to really get to know this God whom I had rejected.

But my feelings for my husband were still packed on ice. I knew how God felt about divorce, but I didn't see how the marriage could survive. If I agreed to reconcile, could God give me back the feelings? If He didn't, could I endure without them?

It was at that point that God showed me something about faith. Noah didn't know if the rains would ever come, but he went ahead and built the ark. That was faith. Moses didn't know where he was leading those thousands of Israelites, but he led them. That was faith. Mary didn't know what would become of her when she agreed to be the mother of the Son of God, but she did it anyway. That was faith. None of these people knew the outcome of their obedience, but they did it anyway because that is faith. They were willing to be willing, to face the unknown, because they knew that the One they obeyed is faithful.

And so my husband and I reconciled. It wasn't an overnight miracle. It has been up and down, good and sometimes pretty bad. But God has been faithful. When I look back at those times before, during and after our separation, I no longer see hopelessness, pain and despair. I see God.

My husband called me from a business trip last night. "Love you," he said after wishing me good night.

"I love you too," I replied. And you know, I really do!

Father God, thank You for Your love which never gives up. Please melt the icy spots in my heart so that Your living water might flow through me. In Jesus' name, Amen.

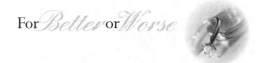

Love Is Not an Accident

Edward E. Menaldino

But God demonstrates his own love for us in this: While we were still sinners, Christ died for us. (Romans 5:8)

He had yet to meet the wife chosen by his parents when he asked, "Will you marry us, Pastor?" After some hesitancy, not wanting to cause cultural or social confusion, the pastor agreed. Several months after the marriage, the couple said, "You probably want to know if we really love each other. Well, we do very much, because we chose to love each other."

That's it; that's real love; that is divine love! My commitment to God is not generated by sentimental love but by a rational choice, which in turn results in a profound affection for a God I have not yet seen. Peter caught the full significance of this principle in First Peter 1:8: "You love him even though you have never seen him; though not seeing him, you trust him; and even now you are happy with the inexpressible joy that comes from heaven itself" (TLB).

While visiting India, where parents choose the husbands and wives for their children, I asked, very discreetly, if there exists true love between husbands and wives when love was not an initial factor in the unions. They reminded me that in America, where falling in love is the primary factor for marriage, the divorce rate is over fifty percent; in India divorce is a very uncommon event. They reminded me that love is an act of the will.

True love is not a matter of falling in or out of love. Falling is an accident; accidents rarely turn out positive. We are not victims of love but the administrators of love. The victim concept relieves us of personal responsibility or liability for our behavior, but at the same time it removes any virtue, credit or meaning from love when circumstances are convenient.

In true affection, neither the giver nor the recipient is a victim of emotional accidents. Each participates in the very highest and noblest act of the will—*giving*!

> *Lord, You have provided us all we need to love: Your Word, a new birth with a spiritual disposition, Your indwelling presence by the Holy Spirit, Your promise to direct the affairs of our lives. Help us choose to forgive, to heal and to love. Reconcile us to You and to one another. Amen.*

PART THREE

For Richer, for Poorer

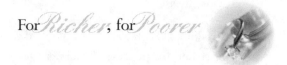

From Dimes to Destiny

Lee Roddy

*Remember how the LORD your God led you all the way . . . to test you
in order to know what was in your heart.* (Deuteronomy 8:2)

In great mental anguish, I showed my wife a glass tube containing a few dollars' worth of dimes. That's all the money we had. There was no food in the house—which was about to be repossessed. The Internal Revenue Service had seized our small bank account. There was no income and none in sight. What really hurt me was that this bleak financial hole seemed to be the result of my stepping out in faith to write for the Lord.

For nearly forty years before that, I had worked hard, serving some of the nation's largest corporations. Cicely and I were never rich, but I had made enough money to live comfortably, pay our bills and put our two children through college. Then, with Cicely's blessing, I had left the business world to pursue a lifelong dream to write books.

While working on my books, I earned short-term income by writing or editing for eighty national or international Christian leaders or their ministries. Gradually some of my books sold, but they didn't earn enough for our basic needs. Cicely and I began sliding down an economic abyss. Desperately but vainly I sought to sell more of my work as the dimes silently mocked me.

At our wedding, Cicely and I had pledged to live our lives together "for richer, for poorer." I increasingly felt crushed emotionally as we were helplessly sucked down into an ever-widening spiritual maelstrom of debt and doubt. I was also humiliated because now, in later life, we were down to those dimes. Cicely deserved better.

I repeatedly agonized in prayer. I pointed out that I had thought I was doing what the Lord wanted me to do. Had I been wrong? Had I trusted in vain?

There seemed to be no answer as we hit bottom and then crashed right on through it.

Our time of testing suddenly changed. A major Christian publisher offered me a contract to write a series of books for young readers. That was the turnaround.

I wrote rapidly, producing three books annually. More than sixty have now been published. A few million copies have sold. They made the best-seller lists and were distributed in nineteen foreign countries.

Looking back, those dimes remind me of how the Lord led us. Cicely and I are very grateful that He has since given us much more than we ever had before.

> *Father, You know how reluctant I am to share this personal experience, but I do so in the hope that it encourages those who are similarly tested. "For richer, for poorer," may they take hope and persevere. Amen.*

Scrambled, Fried or Over Easy

Diane Mitchell

Thou hast caused men to ride over our heads; we went through fire and through water: but thou broughtest us out into a wealthy place. (Psalm 66:12, KJV)

Bankruptcy at age fifty was a frightening prospect. A promising small business venture did not produce the yield that had looked to be a pretty good wager. All of our eggs had gone into that one basket, but long hours and hard work over a three-year period only produced a batch of broken eggs.

Fortunately we had learned the principle, "When life hands you a lemon, make lemonade." Only now we could make an omelette!

All we had worked for over the years—our savings, our house, our credit rating, our retirement and our good name—were all wrapped up in that "shell" that became so fragile it cracked. There we stood with egg on our faces!

Where do we go from here? we wondered.

A friend gave me a poster that read, "Never be afraid to trust an unknown future to a known God." Amen!

We are just on the other side of bankruptcy, so I cannot tell you all life has yet to hold, but I can tell you my husband and I, as a couple, are in the best place we have ever been in as far as our relationship is concerned.

I believe a great deal of this has to do with not blaming or laying a guilt trip on anyone, but rather accepting that we needed to bless God and each other in good times *and* in times that are not so good. God knows! That is security in and of itself. We don't have to face our middle or older years with fear of the future. We can simply learn new recipes for eggs!

God, thank You for teaching us to place our trust in things eternal when our security in the things of this world is cracked. Are there skillets in heaven? Do You like scrambled eggs? Amen.

Money Matters

Jean M. Olsen

Give, and it will be given to you. A good measure, pressed down,
shaken together and running over, will be poured into your lap. For
with the measure you use, it will be measured to you. (Luke 6:38)

Many couples have major arguments over money, but my husband
and I have never fought over finances. That must be a modern-day
miracle, because he tends to be a saver, while I enjoy spending.
What saved us from clashes over cash?

We were determined to keep our wedding vows—to stick together "for richer, for poorer." And we fully expected to be
poorer, for we were headed to the mission field where we would
live in the wilds of Africa on a low income with no malls, credit
cards or catalogs to tantalize us. We spent only what we had, and
we made up our minds to be content.

I'd already had some practice economizing. In Bible college I
received $12 a week for working afternoons in the school office.
I gave God ten percent, or $1.20. After paying $10 for room and
board, I had $.80 to spend. I learned to economize, but I never
suffered. Jesus said, "Give, and it will be given to you," and He
kept His promise.

On our furloughs in the United States, our missionary salary
was below the poverty level. Our children even qualified for free
lunches. Yet we never lacked any good thing. As we began each

new assignment in Africa, God, through His people, supplied all we needed to return overseas.

Twice, during civil wars in Sudan and Zaire, we lost all our belongings. But God replaced them. When our children finished high school, they attended good colleges. Overcome with awe, we saw them graduate free of debt. My bookkeeper husband could never quite explain how that happened.

Several years ago, as we contemplated all God had given us, we felt bad that we were still giving him only a tithe. So we began increasing our tithe by one percent each year. As always, God has given us all we need and more. We're buying our first house, and we're living more comfortably on seventy-five percent than we used to on ninety percent!

Lord, thank You for making us rich in things that matter most. Amen.

Marriage is a precious gift from God, a

message of just how much He loves us.

—J. L. Hardesty

Rest for the Weary

Karen O'Connor

Come to me, all you who are weary and burdened, and I will give you rest. (Matthew 11:28)

One year while my husband was establishing a new career, I took advantage of an opportunity to earn some additional money to tide us over. But the strain of keeping everything going—our home, family, church work and my usual writing and teaching—began to get to me. I was suddenly fed up with my self-appointed role as "Super Wife."

"Dear Lord," I prayed one day as I flew home from an exhausting two-week consulting job out of state, "You know my needs and the needs of my home and family. I can't do it all. What about Charles? Isn't it time for him to bring in some money? It seems like the burden is all mine! I need help!"

I arrived home later that day ready to speak with my husband about the resentment building up inside me. I wanted him to do something about it! Imagine my surprise when I walked into a sparkling clean kitchen and bathroom and a newly painted living room, dining room and hallway. Every picture and painting on our walls (and we have a collection to rival a small museum!) and every dish and glass in the china cabinet had been washed and re-placed. The silverware was tarnish-free. The furniture throughout the house was freshly oiled, and the carpets had been perfectly vacuumed.

"Just wanted to surprise you," Charles said, smiling from ear to ear. "If you can help with the earnings for a while, it's the least I can do to help with the chores around here. Welcome home, honey! I missed you."

I glanced heavenward and whispered a humble, "Thanks!"

I wrapped my arms around my husband. "I appreciate you so much," I whispered in his ear. Then I headed for the kitchen, ready to prepare his favorite meal. My grumbling had given way to gratitude.

Dear Lord, thank You for Your steadfast love and Your faithful mercy throughout my marriage. This experience reminds me once again that You are the center of our marriage, the One who promises never to leave nor forsake us—no matter what! Amen.

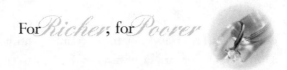

Putting God First

Kathleen Hayes

From everyone who has been given much, much will be demanded; and from the one who has been entrusted with much, much more will be asked. (Luke 12:48)

When my husband and I met, I was living in an apartment in what was considered a bad neighborhood, making a "simple" living as a freelance editor and writer. His mother had advised him that since there were both rich and poor women in the world, he may as well go for a rich one! Despite the advice, he fell in love with me.

As our relationship deepened, Jeff and I revealed that we had about the same modest amount in savings. (We used to joke that by marrying we would double our assets.) What I didn't tell him until after our engagement was that I would inherit a generous amount of money upon my father's death. Two years into our marriage, that inheritance became a reality.

Being financially secure certainly has its advantages. At the same time, money is an awesome responsibility and frequent stumbling block for Christians. Consider the many biblical admonitions: we cannot serve both God and money (Matthew 6:24; Luke 16:13); we are to seek first the kingdom of God (Matthew 6:33); we are to lay up our treasures in heaven (6:19-20).

All of us "who are rich in this present world" (1 Timothy 6:17), which includes most North Americans, must ask what the Lord requires of us financially. For those couples who inherit significant sums of money or earn high wages, it is crucial to talk freely and pray often about how to use that money. The same is true for those who live from paycheck to paycheck. Mutually agreed upon goals for giving, saving and spending can help establish trust, and joint knowledge about the family's finances nurtures honesty.

Contentment in marriage grows out of trusting God together to meet every need—financial or otherwise. Are you struggling to make ends meet? Lay up your treasures in heaven, and God will meet your needs. Have you been given much in earthly riches? If so, God requires much of you, including generosity and joyful service to others, especially the poor. No matter what our financial situation, God must be first. Whether our marriages are for richer or for poorer, they are to be built on our pursuit of God, not wealth.

Lord, help us to love You more than anything else. We want to keep our finances in perspective, be generous in giving and be content with whatever we have. In Jesus' holy name, Amen.

Marriage on a Dollar a Day
Clint Kelly

A man's riches may ransom his life, but a poor man hears no threat.
(Proverbs 13:8)

The car I drive is a twenty-four-year-old clunker. Nobody steals it because, frankly, nobody wants it.

I'm no fan of poverty, but it has its advantages. When you have little, few people want the little you have.

But that's not what I told my bride of a year when I suggested we go to Canada to each work for a dollar a day. No, I think I said something more like, "Snow! Ice hockey! A foreign country! What an adventure, eh?"

The employer was a Christian lay order that ran boarding schools. We would help teach and operate the schools. Along with our colleagues, we would live in campus housing, eat company food, use company vehicles and be paid an individual wage of one dollar a day. Instant equality!

But we were young marrieds with one child and another on the way. How to stretch our combined $2 a day plus a small monthly child support stipend from the government?

It meant we really had to pull together as a family. Date nights at the drive-in were in a car with a fold-down backseat so the kids could sleep while we watched the late-night movie and avoided babysitting fees. An "amusement park" for us was the free city park where the playground equipment became an obstacle course and the kids competed to see who could complete the course in the best time. Plates of frosted cookies and zucchini bread tied up in bows were our Christmas gifts to others.

We weren't always satisfied with less. Some gifts and vacations had to be deferred. Long-distance phone calls to family in the States were kept short. We didn't eat out a lot. But we discovered that contentment is a state of heart and mind. It's focusing on what you have, not dwelling on what you lack. It's finding fun in the challenge of making something last, or making it over into something new.

The day our salaries jumped to $2 a day each, we didn't quite know what to do. Sudden wealth can be such a burden!

Oh Lord, help me find contentment with whatever I've been given. Thank You for my wife, who shows me daily that without cost I can always laugh more, love more, give more of me. Keep my eyes on Jesus, who owned little and gave everything. Amen.

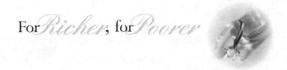

You Can't Take It with You

Lynn D. Morrissey

Do not store up for yourselves treasures on earth, where moth and rust destroy, and where thieves break in and steal. (Matthew 6:19)

I fumed out of the house, spouting angry words at my poor, patient husband. "That's it! I'm not putting up with a used car breaking down one more time! I want a new one!"

Headed for work in my decrepit Mustang, I regretted the words I'd vented at Michael, yet I felt justified, stubbornly holding my ground. After all, I worked, and I deserved decent transportation. We would just have to make the budget stretch somehow. I didn't want a "better" used car. I wanted the best—a new one! I refused to be in a position to have to worry incessantly over repairs.

Just then, a large trailer passed me on the highway, transporting a colorful array of new cars. They sparkled in the sun like jewels, and I coveted them. Literally seconds later, a similar trailer passed, hauling rusted wrecks to the recycler.

In that fleeting moment, God gave me an object lesson in establishing values and trusting my husband's wisdom. Why was I "spinning my wheels" when even the "lilies of the field" didn't spin, labor or worry? God provided for them and even for the birds of the air. Wouldn't He provide for my needs too? Why was I worrying over material things that would eventually be destroyed and wouldn't accompany me to heaven anyway?

That day I asked my husband's forgiveness and prayed that God would change my heart to value things of eternal worth. I still haven't bought a new car, and I haven't regretted it for a minute!

Lord, help me to stop pressuring my husband over money. He is a wonderful provider, but You are my true provider. You will supply my needs, though You may not always provide my wants. Lord, one thing I do need is to become a lily; then I won't labor, spin, worry or argue. With Your provision, I will simply grow in grace. Amen.

An Embarrassment of Riches

Bonnie Doran

Moreover, when God gives any man wealth and possessions, and enables him to enjoy them, to accept his lot and be happy in his work—this is a gift of God. (Ecclesiastes 5:19)

"My husband and I have a great arrangement with money," I quipped to a friend. "He makes it, and I spend it!"

Although I said this tongue-in-cheek, I do spend considerable time (and money) in the shopping malls. John makes a generous salary; his seven-year-old business is successful and lucrative.

Many of our friends are struggling financially, which makes our situation a bit awkward. Most are happy with our success, but a few are envious and resentful. I sometimes feel embarrassed by riches.

We talk about how God will meet our material needs. But what happens when God's abundance is poured into our laps? Can we actually enjoy God's financial blessings without feeling guilty?

I believe we can, but with caution.

Keeping our financial situation in perspective takes work, whether we have a little or a lot. That perspective comes as we recognize God's control in everything, including our bottom line. If we're broke, we trust Him to meet our needs. If we are blessed with abundance, we enjoy it as a gift from His hand.

We are blessed at this time with a large amount of disposable income. Of course, it hasn't always been this way. I remember cashing in the penny jar for pocket money. Once we dined for free at a fast-food restaurant, courtesy of strip mall coupons we won in a costume contest.

Money conflicts in our marriage did not disappear with affluence. We have different views on spending, saving and giving. We need wisdom and compromise, whether the discussion centers around $10 or $1,000.

It's like the decision I made when John wanted a new pet: "All right, you can have a snake, but I draw the line at tarantulas!" I need to let John enjoy his new ham radio receiver, but it doesn't have to be the most expensive model. He needs to let me enjoy my new dress, but I don't need designer fashions. We need to keep each other balanced and accountable without spoiling the fun.

Money shouldn't put us in a tug-of-war with each other. Rather, we should pull in the same direction as we recognize our joint responsibility under God to use His blessings wisely and joyfully.

Father, thank You for Your financial blessings. Help us to be good stewards of the abundance You've given us. Amen.

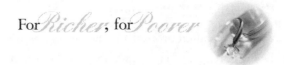

Now What Do We Do?

Marjorie Geary Vawter

And my God will liberally supply (fill to the full) your every need according to His riches in glory in Christ Jesus. (Philippians 4:19, AMP)

"Mom, if I could drive, I could save you time and gas running Randy and me to school," my daughter, Kathy, announced as she pulled out her strongest argument yet as to why she should start driving. It took forty-five minutes, one way, to drive them to school.

"I know that. But we'd have to pay insurance on you and we can't afford it. You better keep praying," was my reply.

End of discussion—one of many we'd had in the year since we had pulled up roots from our Illinois home and moved to Colorado. The Lord had clearly directed us to leave a comfortable home, excellent jobs and a strong church family to become the directors of a small church camp in the foothills of the Rocky Mountains. In obeying, we were forced to rely on Him for even the basic necessities of life—things we took for granted before. Since we were now paid about one-third of our previous income, many things we had perceived as needs before were now put on a waiting list. And our family prayer time became much more specific.

I had done some research on the driving issue. In Colorado, driver's education is not required to get a license, but our insurance company gives a discount for those who go through driver's training. I called around to the various driving schools in the Denver area and found the cheapest was about $250—way out of our range at that time. So Kathy was forced to wait—and pray.

A few weeks later, a woman in our church asked us to join her for a Christmas celebration at a local restaurant. We willingly accepted, grateful for the gift of a nice meal cooked by someone else. She surprised us with more generous gifts at the end of the meal. In Kathy's card was $200 to use for driver's education.

Do I regret leaving Illinois with its abundance and coming to Colorado, following my husband? No. Our marriage, and our family, are stronger today because of it. I wouldn't trade that for all the riches in the world.

Father, You have promised to provide all our needs through Jesus Christ. And You have proved faithful to that promise more than once. I thank You. Amen.

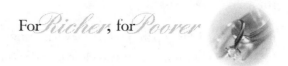

Critters, Cages and
Not Much Cash

Linda J. White

He himself bore our sins in his body on the tree, so that we might die
to sins and live for righteousness; by his wounds you have been healed.
(1 Peter 2:24)

True love often can't wait for financial stability! Like many a
starry-eyed couple, Larry and I began our marriage with full
hearts and empty wallets. Our first home was an efficiency apartment on Connecticut Avenue in Washington, D.C., located just
a block from the National Zoological Park.

Cheap entertainment was a necessity. We took advantage of the
free-admission zoo by taking a walk there every night. We never
seemed to tire of watching Bill and Lucy, the white rhinos, or the
sprightly Dorcas gazelle. Hand in hand we'd stroll down the paths,
delighting in new arrivals, greeting old friends and enjoying each
other's company.

One night we found ourselves on a "side street" at the zoo,
fascinated by the zebras and the gnus. At some point, I noticed
that we were all alone. "It's getting late," I said.

I held my new husband's arm as we walked back toward the exit.
He was still cracking jokes about "g-news." *How odd*, I thought to
myself as we merged onto a bigger path. No one else was in sight;
there were no visitors, no vendors, no security guards. "Let's go,

hon," I said, picking up the pace. After what seemed like an eternity, we reached the main gate. It was closed. And secured.

We were locked in the zoo! A sign announcing a change in closing time beginning that day hung on the fence.

"Larry, what are we going to do?" My mind was racing. *Do they really let the lions loose at night*, I wondered, *or is that just my imagination?*

"The car gate!" he said. "That's probably not closed."

We broke into a jog and ran down the main path, past the buildings, back into Gnu Alley. The zebras looked up curiously as we went by. But the car gate was closed—closed and locked.

Already I could see the headlines: "Couple Found Mauled in Zoo." "Overnight Stay Lands Pair in Lockup."

That's when we noticed the tree. A large maple stood next to the drive. One of its sturdy branches extended over the fence. Could we do it? We were young; we were intrepid. Within moments we were scrambling up the trunk. We crawled out on the branch, past the fence and dropped to the ground. Free at last!

Some years later, we would discover another tree, the tree that Jesus hung on when He freed us from bondage to sin and death. But that night we were thankful just to get out of the zoo.

Father, we thank You that You provide a way of escape. Jesus was crucified on a tree to save us from condemnation and allow us to have eternal life. Thank You for giving us the opportunity to be saved through faith in Jesus Christ. Amen.

The Girls Need Shoes

Jim Dyet

And we know that in all things God works for the good of those who love him, who have been called according to his purpose. (Romans 8:28)

When President Lyndon B. Johnson declared war on poverty, I thought my wife, Gloria, and I would be taken prisoner within thirty days! We were living from hand to mouth in the mid-1960s. Fortunately, it was God's hand and our mouths, but my $3,000 pastor's salary didn't go far. At times operating my car for pastoral visits cut into household expenses, and winter heating bills were about as welcome as incoming artillery shells. Our marriage was definitely in the "for poorer" stage of our wedding vows. We wondered when the "for richer" stage would begin.

"The girls need shoes," Gloria reminded me one day. Our daughters, Sherrie and Heather, were then four and two (ages, not shoe sizes). Being a resourceful person, Gloria also reminded me that a pastor's magazine offered $1 for every sermon outline submitted and published. "Why don't you send them ten outlines?" she asked.

Two days later ten sermon outlines were in the mail. Fourteen days later I received a check for $10. The girls got their shoes, and I got a taste for writing. After submitting additional sermon outlines and having them published, I queried the editor with an idea for an article. He approved, and I wrote "Teach Teens to Preach." That was the first of hundreds of articles that followed in a variety of publications.

Eight years after writing the sermon outlines, a curriculum publisher in Denver, Colorado, invited me to join its editorial staff. I accepted. Now, thirty years later, I look back on a much wider ministry than the one I had when I entered the career of writing and editing. I have contributed to five lines of curriculum, written more than thirty Bible study courses and authored several books. Truly the Lord used a simple need to direct me into an extensive ministry and to demonstrate His goodness to Gloria and me.

Although we have been married for forty-three years and the girls buy their own shoes now, I plan to keep writing until either the rapture occurs or I buy a shoe company.

> *Lord, thank You for providing for every need and for a marriage that has survived times of need. I thank You for taking a little bit of writing talent and using it to bless many, just as You took a little boy's lunch and used it to satisfy 5,000 appetites. Amen.*

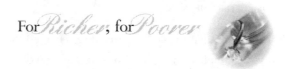

The Perfect Table

Carolyn Woodie

The borrower is servant to the lender. (Proverbs 22:7)

As newlyweds, we lived from paycheck to paycheck. We tried to spend wisely and save for purchases rather than use credit. Often one-half of our twosome was more disciplined about such matters than the other. OK, I admit it—I was the one who found it easier to spend than to save.

At one point I was convinced we needed a new dining table. After my extremely logical arguments, my husband agreed and I excitedly scoured the furniture ads. I finally found a great table for a reasonable price. We both thought that we had enough money saved for the purchase, so that following Saturday we headed out to shop.

The table was perfect. It would work really well with our furniture. We made arrangements to pay cash on delivery. On the way home, I envisioned joyful meals with friends around our new table.

After we got home, my husband checked our savings and said, "Oh no, we don't have enough money to pay for it."

"Well, I guess we'll just have to charge it," I said.

"We'll have to cancel the order," he responded matter-of-factly. "Remember, we agreed not to go into additional debt right now."

I couldn't believe it! I tried every logic in the book to convince him otherwise. He was taking this agreement entirely too literally! Hadn't we given our word to the salesman that we were purchasing the table? What would it matter if we charged the table and paid it off in a couple of months? But nothing would sway him.

It was my job to cancel the order. Down deep, I knew it was best not to go into debt, but it was very hard for me to call the salesman. I was humiliated with a capital "H" and angry with my husband to top it off.

Eventually we did get a new table similar to the original one, and we paid cash. We used it in several of our homes and, in fact, passed it on to our son and his wife to help furnish their first home. Each time I see the table, I am reminded of the incident and of my husband's wisdom. Over the years, we have been truly blessed by his consistent, not-easily-swayed management of our finances.

Dear Lord, thank You for the sensible and disciplined husband You have given me to balance my sometimes impetuous habits. Help me to appreciate his wisdom and consistency. Use him to help make me into the person You want me to be. Amen.

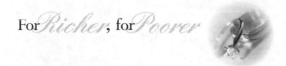

The Day the Bulldozers Showed Up

Terry Martin

But seek first the kingdom of God and His righteousness, and all these
things shall be added to you. (Matthew 6:33, NKJV)

Some years ago we bought a lovely hillside property in northern California surrounded by six acres of redwood forest. We knew there were problems left to us by the previous owners, but the property was a really good deal, so we went ahead. The problems were complicated and had been in the courts for many years. A neighbor had sued the previous owners over an easement and through various court decisions now had a claim on the property. It was being appealed in the courts by the former owners, but we knew that if the neighbor won the suit, we'd be the ones who had to live with the consequences.

We enjoyed the property for almost two years, and then the courts finally made a decision. The lawsuit against the previous owners wound up going against them, and the neighbor got the title to the property, voiding our title. Although he let us stay there for a couple of months while we were moving, the first thing he did was bring in bulldozers and demolish the prettiest part of the hillside.

Having bulldozers in your front yard can put a lot of stress on your marriage, to say the least! It was frustrating, but that first day, as I ranted and raved about unjust judges and inept attorneys, my husband started laughing. Furious, I asked him how he could possibly laugh, and he said, "That guy thinks he took something away from us, but he didn't. It wasn't ours anyway. It was the Lord's. We got to live in a great place for a while, and now He's moving us somewhere else. It doesn't matter. God's in control."

He got out his Bible and read Matthew 6:33. I realized I hadn't been doing what it said. I hadn't been seeking first His kingdom. I'd been focused on a couple of acres of dirt. I needed to readjust my focus and seek the things that mattered, not the things that didn't.

As we went through that stressful time, we kept reminding each other of that verse and encouraged (and sometimes nagged) each other to keep our focus on the kingdom, not on the dirt. It wasn't always easy. I did my share of fussing and fuming, but we got through it with our marriage stronger than ever.

Soon afterward we moved to another state. I sometimes miss those redwoods, but I have a view of the Rocky Mountains that can't be beat. Every time I see those mountains, I remember the rest of the promise: "All these things shall be added unto you" (Matthew 6:33, KJV).

Father God, help me to keep my focus on Your kingdom and not on the dirt; help me to trust in Your provision for my needs instead of worrying when the bulldozers are digging up the hillside. In Jesus' name, Amen.

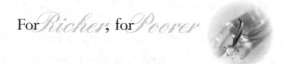

We Will Trust in Him

Barbara Hibschman

*For this God is our God for ever and ever; he will be our guide even to
the end.* (Psalm 48:14)

You know you're getting older when your children make humorous comments about your black-and-white wedding photos.

"That's how they did it in 1964," I explained.

"Mom, look at your poofy hair, and you're thin! Dad looks like Eddie Haskell on that old TV show *Leave It to Beaver.*"

There's no denying that we've changed. (That's a nice way of saying we've aged over the last thirty-eight years.) Yes, we've aged, gained a few pounds and earned a few wrinkles.

"Here, look at this one. This is my favorite wedding picture," I said as I flipped through the wedding album pages. The response was one of laughter at my odd sense of humor. Our faces were not in the picture. It only showed our joined hands on an open Bible covering our chosen "life verse" for our marriage, Psalm 48:14. It reads, "For this God is our God for ever and ever; he will be our guide even to the end."

There may be a few wrinkles on our hands now, but it is my favorite wedding picture because even though we've changed, God hasn't. Everything God says in His Word is true. It will come to pass. We have chosen to trust Him for all our days, and

He will be our guide. Our God IS, and because He IS, He is the source of all we've needed and will ever need.

The day we chose Psalm 48:14 as our marriage verse, we had no idea or understanding of the outpouring of love we would experience as we trusted in our God, the provider of all our needs.

In the years to come, as we put our trust in Him, we will continue to learn and accept in times of want, adversity and uncontrollable circumstances that He is God and we are not! Therefore, He has the right to change our plans, to move us and use us where He guides and leads. We willfully choose to trust in Him, for He is our God.

Heavenly Father, we bow down and worship You for being our guide and provider—for being a God who is all we have ever needed and all we will ever need. Help us to choose to trust You for all the needs we face today and to rest in Your sufficiency. In Jesus' name, Amen.

PART FOUR

In Sickness and Health

In Sickness . . .

Jana Carman

Do you not know? Have you not heard? The LORD . . . gives strength to the weary. (Isaiah 40:28-29)

The bride looked startled as she opened my shower gift. Tucked in a plastic box were a thermometer, a box of bandages, a tube of burn ointment, a sickroom bell, aspirin and several medicine cabinet kinds of things that every household needs sooner or later.

"Love is not always glamorous, but it will help you get to the bathroom when you're sick," Helen Woodhall wrote in an open letter to her granddaughter in *Guideposts* magazine. It also helps you mop up when someone doesn't make it there in time, or go out in the middle of the night for cough medicine, or change bandages or sheets again and again.

Most of us going into marriage have had no worse ailment than a broken bone or a bad case of the flu. Serious illness or injury is something that happens to other people. It never occurred to me that our family would experience the heartbreak and upheaval of mental illness, yet over a period of fifteen years we coped with four separate hospitalizations for extended times.

Sometimes *coped* was barely the word. Each time John and I suffered together as his depression became more severe. Each time the agonizing decision to go back to the hospital had to be made—or was made for us by a crisis. And each time we struggled together as John climbed that steep hill back to health.

It was during one of the crisis times that I leaned against my father and cried, "Daddy, I don't know how I can take any more."

He may have felt like he was mouthing an empty cliché, but he said what I needed: "Take it one day at a time."

Someone has said that none of us can carry a lifetime's burden, but we can each carry this hour's worth. "Your strength will equal your days" (Deuteronomy 33:25).

> *O Lord, You alone are my strength. Pick me up when I collapse. Comfort me in pain. Carry me in weakness. Infuse me with Your power to go on. Thank You for staying close. Amen.*

I Do

Martha Marlow Carpenter

If a man makes a vow to the LORD, or takes an oath to bind himself with a binding obligation, he shall not violate his word; he shall do according to all that proceeds out of his mouth. (Numbers 30:2, NASB)

On June 28, 1991, I watched as hundreds of soldiers home from the Persian Gulf War marched across a parade field in Ft. Stewart, Georgia. Somewhere in the crowd, dressed in desert camouflage, was my husband. After months of separation, our lives could finally return to normal.

Sadly, normal was not to be.

Before we left Ft. Stewart, I realized Bill was not well. Coughing incessantly, he suffered excruciating chest, muscle and joint pain and had difficulty breathing. My husband, who was able to run two miles with a full military pack when he left for Saudi Arabia, could not walk up a flight of stairs or do simple chores.

As months passed, the military disregarded his pleas for help. Instead his condition was diagnosed as post-traumatic stress, age-related or psychological illness and laziness. Finally, a year after his return, Bill applied for disability leave from his job, and we increased our attempts to get help from the military.

One night, as we lay in bed talking, he spoke hesitantly of the future.

"Honey . . . we don't know how bad this thing is going to get."
His voice was soft. "I mean, it's bad enough, but still . . ." He didn't
finish the thought.

I rolled over on my side and placed my hand on his chest. Even
though he was propped up against several pillows, his breathing was
labored.

"No matter how bad it gets, Bill, we'll see it through with the
Lord's help."

He lay quietly for a moment. "What I'm trying to say is that it
may get more difficult for you. I mean . . . I might get . . . bedridden, you know, not able to take care of myself."

My eyes filled with tears. My husband was asking for reassurance
that I would not "bolt and run." Could I handle it? What if . . . ?

Taking a deep breath, I placed my hand on his cheek and spoke
firmly. "Bill, I am here for the duration, even if I have to care for you
like a baby. By the grace of God, I will not leave you, ever."

I have recalled my vow many times during the last ten years. Bill
is not bedridden, but his condition has worsened. Fatigue and discouragement have stalked me, and God has led me through anger
and grief, but always in my heart are the words of that night.

In a significant and personal way, God taught me about "in
sickness and in health" and asked me again if I meant it. By His
grace, I do.

> *Thank You for the strength and wisdom to meet the needs of my fam-*
> *ily. Help me today to respond to them according to Your love in me.*
> *Amen.*

God's Grace

Vickie Phelps

And he said unto me, My grace is sufficient for thee: for my strength is made perfect in weakness. (2 Corinthians 12:9, KJV)

My fingers ached from the constant massaging of my husband's right shoulder and arm, but I continued rubbing and caressing the inflamed area. The rotator cuff surgery had repaired the damage but left him with excruciating pain to deal with daily. The massage would give him a couple of hours of relief.

As I worked, I thought about all the physical problems Sonny had endured.

Three months before we took our vows, he underwent bypass surgery to open blocked arteries and prolong his life. From then on, it became an endless stream of visits to one specialist or another for back surgery, pain management, foot surgery for tumors, eye surgery for premature cataracts in both eyes and hand surgery on both hands at the same time for carpal tunnel syndrome. Every year for the past three years he had gone back to the hospital to have heart procedures performed—and now the shoulder problem that left him exhausted and edgy from dealing with the pain.

I remembered an early-morning incident two years ago. We awoke and lay in bed talking.

"Why did you have to get me in my bad years?" Sonny asked. "Why couldn't you have come along sooner?"

"I don't know," I said, although I had been guilty of wondering the same thing. I didn't regret our marriage; I just wished for good health for my husband.

Later, looking back on that conversation, I decided God must have sent me along when I was needed most. God teaches us through our experiences, and perhaps I needed to learn dependence on Him for grace in trying times as much as Sonny needed an understanding mate.

We will soon celebrate seventeen years of marriage. It hasn't always been easy, but it's been blessed by God. We have experienced His grace and strength through every medical procedure Sonny has endured. God's grace has made it possible for us to face every situation as one.

Jesus, thank You for Your amazing grace, which enables us to endure every circumstance. Amen.

Marriage is not so much excitement as

it is tenderness and comfort.

—*J.L. Hardesty*

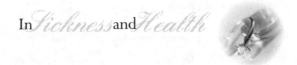

Victory Despite Disease

Candy Arrington

He took up our infirmities and carried our diseases. (Matthew 8:17)

"Just get away from me. Back off! Don't touch me!"

His voice echoed around the restaurant. Although his words were irrational, I was totally embarrassed. My husband was in the throes of a hypoglycemic reaction and was combative regarding my attempts to help him. For an insulin-pump-dependent, type 1 diabetic, blood glucose balance is a daily battle. When hypoglycemia occurs, he becomes a different person. It is but one of the complications of diabetes.

When Jim and I married, his disease was in the early stages. I loved him. So he had diabetes! So what? In my bride-mind, I thought taking shots and eating right was all that was necessary. The emotional impact of diabetes is what blindsided me. I was unprepared for personality changes and withdrawal. The feelings of defensiveness, anger and defeat my husband experiences often keep him in an emotional tailspin. The emotions are complicated. Depression lurks.

Ultimately diabetes affects our relationship because it is an invasive, neverending part of our marriage. All aspects of the disease, including potential kidney failure, blindness, nerve damage and hypoglycemia, as well as monitoring and a bathroom counter full of preventative medications, are frightening.

Several years ago a hypoglycemic reaction almost took my husband's life. The flashing blue light and mangled wreck of the car are forever etched in my memory. God miraculously intervened, and Jim walked away from the wreckage.

As a newlywed, I didn't know Jim would face retinal hemorrhages, temporary blindness and eye surgeries. I didn't know we would have to work really hard to maintain emotional intimacy. Would I have chosen to marry him if I had known? YES! Love doesn't end because circumstances are difficult. Even though the "or worse" is harder than expected, there are many good things about our relationship. God is faithful to ease our fears and give us joyous moments amid the struggles.

There is no cure or quick fix for diabetes on earth, but praise God that the cure for sin, illness and death was settled long ago on the cross. Though the battle to recognize the victory rages on, the war is already won.

Father, I thank You for calming our fears and strengthening us in our infirmities. I rest in the confidence that You are in control no matter what the future holds. Amen.

Looking Beyond

Jeannie Harmon

But one thing I do, forgetting those things which are behind and reaching forward to those things which are ahead, I press toward the goal for the prize of the upward call of God in Christ Jesus. (Philippians 3:13-14, NKJV)

We have always been a mismatched couple. He rises early. I sleep late. He likes to sit in the woods and ponder. I like to travel and cram every possible moment with exciting happenings. He drives a pickup truck. I drive a minivan.

These are not the critical issues of life. We have learned to compromise our differences, sharing when we can, and sometimes electing to go our separate ways to do what each enjoys. However, there is one difference for which there is no compromise. He is healthy and I am not.

Through the years I have struggled with a chronic disease that has its ups and downs. He plays the role of the sick person's spouse—trying to be empathetic, trying to help when he can, trying to field questions from concerned others and always praying for a solution. There is no manual for his job. Sometimes he feels like we are really moving forward; other times things seem hopeless. Without the stability of our faith, life would seem like a giant roller coaster.

Ten years ago, after a series of foot problems, a specialist told us that I might not be able to walk for much longer. The news hit us hard—more bad news in the growing list of disappointments. As we drove home, we discussed what God's purpose might be in all of this and where we should go from there.

We stopped for a cup of coffee. As I sat there, the brave front that I had exhibited to that point seemed to melt away in a flood of tears.

My husband sat stirring his coffee. Finally he said, "Won't it be nice when our ability matches our desire?" A simple statement, spoken in confident faith. He was looking over the up-and-down battles of this life to a time when there will be no doctors, no illness, no discouragement. He was looking beyond.

Because of his faith, I was able to look beyond. For a single moment, I was renewed in my resolve to press on to the end. The doctor's words did not come true, but in the face of any crisis I'm reminded of the day when we sat over coffee and looked beyond the present circumstances.

Lord, help me be a person who can look beyond what are the obvious hindrances and see hope for myself and for my spouse. Help me not to dwell on the things I cannot change but to look to You for strength, knowing that all good gifts come from You. Amen.

"I've Got Cancer!"

June Eaton

You turned my wailing into dancing . . . and clothed me with joy.
(Psalm 30:11)

When my husband, Fred, returned home from what should have been a routine doctor's appointment, he lingered a little too long in the hallway hanging up his coat and hat.

"You OK?" I asked.

Slowly he turned away from the coatrack. I saw disbelief in his face and heard it in his voice as he whispered, "I've got cancer!"

Too stunned to answer, I wrapped my arms around him. We clung to each other in a silence punctuated only by our tears.

Then he surprised me. "I guess it's our turn," he said simply, referring to all of our friends who had gone through life-threatening illness. And instead of crying, "Why me?" he went on to recount the many blessings God had given us in our forty years of marriage— our children, our past good health, meaningful work, opportunities for travel, our church family, our friends and, finally, our grandchildren. I had never admired him more than I did at that moment.

Recalling the words from Ruth 1:16, "Where you go I will go," I resolved that he would never again receive such frightening news alone. I would accompany him to every doctor's appointment and be at his side for every test and treatment. I would also pray for him as I had never prayed before.

In the coming months, between the appointments, surgery, treatments and excruciating waits for test results, we arranged simple little pleasures together. We went for long walks to work out our frustrations. We shopped in the mall, went to concerts in the park, joined friends for lunch, frequented the library, the bookstore and the zoo. And during the whole year, we missed only two church services.

As our future came into question, everything in life suddenly became sweeter. Our marriage began to take on deeper meaning. We enjoyed each other with a renewed interest, treasuring the things we had in common and appreciating our differences. We acknowledged each other's good points; our faults became merely endearing traits.

Then, miraculously, after all of the tests and surgeries and radiation treatments, God restored my husband's health. In the process, He showed us which things in life were most important. He turned our time of mourning into a time of joy.

Through the darkest nightmare of our lives, the Lord not only brought us closer together, but He stripped the "worse" from our marriage vows and left only the "better." For that we thank and praise Him forever.

Lord, we give thanks that You are a God who can change darkness into light and sorrow into joy. Amen.

Home—Alone

Miggy Krentel

Shall we indeed accept good from God and not accept adversity? (Job 2:10, NASB)

We sat together like wooden dolls in the doctor's office, together in our misery yet apart, each in his own cocoon of fear. The doctor gave us his one-word diagnosis: Alzheimer's.

I gulped. "How can that be? He has Parkinson's already."

"Alzheimer's usually has three telltale symptoms. One is a resting tremor, the second is the inability to write legibly . . ."

"And the third?" I ventured.

"Often the inability to project one's voice."

The doctor looked at the carpet; Paul and I looked at each other.

On the way home in the car, we talked of the future.

"Paul, this will be tough, but we have been through tougher stuff." He smiled wanly at me and looked out the car window.

The ensuing months brought little change, and I began to relax. But then Paul began to do things that made no sense. His disappearing in the neighborhood made me nearly crazy. I did not want to quit my job, but I knew he could no longer be left home alone. His days were long, and TV failed to keep him occupied. Frankly, I did not know where to turn.

When Paul caught me crying quietly one evening, he spoke up. "Are you going to leave me? Put me in a home?"

I threw my arms around him and held him tight. "Honey, how long have we been together? Almost fifty-five years! Did you think somehow that I had forgotten what we said that day so long ago? We vowed to stay together through sickness or health, for better or for worse, 'till death do us part.' "

I held him tighter, all six feet, two inches of him. For the moment he seemed to quiet down.

The days, months and years squeezed together into one long nightmare. Each stage of his disease left me wondering what was next. I was always tired. My nights had turned into his days. But I never could forget the vow I'd made on our wedding day. I knew my Paul would have done the same for me if the situation had been reversed.

Dear God, You have been right here with me, haven't You? Even in those lonely hours during the night—in the good times as well as in those awful times. Father, cover me with Your wings. I can never tell You how much I love You. Amen.

"Oh, My Aching Back!"

Jim Dyet

[Love] always protects, always trusts, always hopes, always perseveres. Love never fails. (1 Corinthians 13:7-8)

One bad golf swing on Labor Day, 2000, hurt not only my score but also my back. Neither pain pills nor spinal injections relieved the horrendous daily pain that bit into my lower back and traveled down the front of my right leg. I was destined to have five hours of surgery on November 30 to repair a lateral herniation, a bone spur and stenosis. The weeks that followed the surgery were better than those that preceded it, but they were no piece of cake. I was able to keep a number of physical therapy appointments, but I couldn't Christmas shop, play golf or walk more than a few yards. A handicap parking permit offered some consolation, but not much for a formerly superactive, young-for-his-years senior citizen.

Fortunately, along with the Lord's unfailing promises, my wife, Gloria, patiently helped me recuperate. She definitely fulfilled the marriage vow to keep me in sickness and in health. She had no way of knowing then that my health was about to take an even bigger turn for the worse.

On February 28, 2001, I suffered a thalamic stroke. My weight dropped dramatically while the number of prescriptions I took increased to six a day. Dizziness, weakness and searing headaches occurred daily. I was too weak even to accompany Gloria to a grocery store or to walk around the block. Through it all, Gloria exhibited patience, hope, love and faith.

Almost a year passed before my strength inched close to what it had been before the stroke. Now I get around quite well and even play golf occasionally. Of course, I keep my eye not only on the ball but also on my back.

Marriage includes cacti as well as roses, rough times as well as good times, tears as well as laughter and shadows as well as sunshine. However, self-sacrificing love for one another will carry a husband and wife through every trial and reflect Christ's love for His Bride, the Church.

Thank You, Lord, that Your love for my wife and me can be reflected in our love for each other—in sickness and in health. Amen.

Marriage is two people traveling together, each one more concerned with the other's well-being than with his or her own.

—J.L. Hardesty

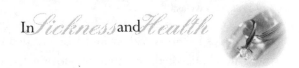

Listen with Our Hearts

Wanda McGlinchey-Ryan

*My dear brothers, take note of this: Everyone should be quick to listen,
slow to speak and slow to become angry.* (James 1:19)

I was unable to speak the words "in sickness and in health"; I was
incapable of this vow. My late husband, Bill, had been a cancer
patient for two and a half years prior to his death. I knew very
well the significance of this pledge. The words caught in my
throat. I needed space. I needed time.

Joe, the new man in my life, was a widower who had lost his
wife to a sudden death. He could not comprehend the magni-
tude of oncologists, radiologists and MRIs. My hesitation to
marry annoyed him. "I do not have that many years left; we are
wasting time," he pleaded.

Joe was impatient. His sister, Catherine, was impatient also;
she wanted him to be happy. She wanted him to be happy *now*.
They would not listen with their hearts. They would not take the
time to absorb the history of my words.

"To have and to hold" and "to love and cherish" held great
appeal. This pledge would be delightful. But "in sickness" was a
responsibility—a responsibility I could not accept. Maybe I
could never say those profound words again.

I had met both men in the same church; that hinted that a
marriage was meant to be. Why, when there are so many un-

happy couples in this world, would I be entitled to the love of two top-notch, devoted, spiritual, fun-loving "characters"?

But I was afraid. I prayed.

I stepped back. I breathed. Alone, away from the pressure, I realized that if Joe became ill I would have wanted to care for him. Marriage would ease, not hamper, that.

So, for the second time in my life, I committed myself. I learned, as the weeks passed, that God's hand certainly touched us. This marriage was made in heaven!

> Let us listen with our hearts to those in turmoil, Lord. Let us hear the pain and feel the history of words spoken. Amen.

Life Was No Picnic

Ginnie Mesibov

Be transformed by the renewing of your mind. (Romans 12:2)

"We're losing him," I overheard the cardiologist tell his nurse.

My husband was lying on a gurney in the emergency room of the local hospital, suffering from a coronary occlusion. The doctor gave him another dose of a new clot-buster drug. It worked. Harold survived his third heart attack.

Life was no picnic in the early years of our marriage. I was the worst person to be married to someone with a severe chronic illness. Handling sickness was not one of my better skills. It was natural for me to panic and overidentify with my husband's problems. When his heart pounded, my heart thumped so loud I could hear it in my ears. When he had difficulty breathing, I gasped for air. Every crippling problem he faced crippled me even more. I knew I couldn't continue like this or I'd be dead long before him—from anxiety alone. I literally had to renew my mind and be transformed. With God's help, I gradually changed my thinking.

I changed how I thought about love. Love does not require me to suffer when Harold is suffering. Love requires me to attend, to take care of and to listen to my husband. Loving objectively allows me to serve him without panic.

I changed how I thought about life. Life is difficult and includes suffering. For some reason, God has allowed severe illness to come into Harold's life and, therefore, into mine. Accepting illness as part of life and as God's will reduces the accompanying anxiety.

I changed how I thought about my husband. Harold is alive! This is my focus. Despite his ill health, he is a vibrant man with an engaging personality who is making a viable contribution to society.

In addition to changing my thinking, I changed my activity: We celebrate! We use any excuse for a party—birthdays, half-birthdays, holidays, anniversaries, good health spurts. . . . Our lives are full.

I also changed how I pray. Now I pray more fervently for my husband's health—his physical, emotional and spiritual health. I pray more earnestly for mine as well, asking God to fill me with His peace. And He has. God is a God who hears and answers prayer.

I'm not a pro at coping with illness; I'm on a learning journey. But today, because of the changes that I made, I can honestly say that life with my beloved husband is a picnic.

Dear God, thank You for helping me to renew my mind. It is by Your power that I am being transformed into a woman who can handle adversity and be at peace. May I continue to trust in Your love, knowing that Your will is best for the both of us. Amen.

Toilet Tissue and Soap Prayers

Carmen Leal

[Love] is not rude, it is not self-seeking, it is not easily angered, it keeps no record of wrongs. (1 Corinthians 13:5)

Folding the laundry, washing dishes, cleaning a toilet or even screwing in a light bulb seemed beyond his ability. It wasn't that he lacked the willingness to help; he simply did an awful job of each chore.

I tried not to be unhappy with my choice of a husband, but little by little I felt the small seed of doubt creep in. It wasn't that I didn't love him or enjoy his company. No, he was a wonderful husband and friend; there were just so many irritating things about him.

It seemed he could not drive without dinging or scraping the car. When he went to the store he inevitably brought home the wrong item. This did not seem like the solid, sensible man I had married.

My husband had been diagnosed with Huntington's disease, so I understood that things would be difficult, yet the growing seeds of discontent had taken hold and were beginning to flourish. I caught the sharp words of rebuke after they slipped from my lips. I listened to my heavy sighs of exasperation and found myself rolling my eyes in disgust.

One morning I prayed that I might accept David and his inabilities. "Please, Lord, give me just one reason to rejoice in my husband."

I dragged myself into the shower where the sharp spray would relax my aching body. I reached for the soap and paused in thought. There are two things I can't stand: One is finding only a sliver of soap once I am wet; the second is finding no toilet paper when I need it. I stood amazed in the shower, realizing God had answered my prayer. I had asked for just one thing that David could still do. In an instant God had shown me two.

In the three years we had been married, I'd never replaced the liquid or bar soap or the toilet tissue. I'd taken for granted that they were always there when I needed them. As much as David couldn't do, there were things he could do. God, knowing my irritations, made provisions for them by giving me a husband who replaced innumerable toilet paper rolls and soap bars.

God's answer to that one small prayer made me a better wife for David, Huntington's and all.

Heavenly Father, continue teaching me to be appreciative of David's abilities instead of keeping a record of his inabilities. Amen.

Hard Lessons

Lenné Kugler-Hunt

[Love] always trusts, always hopes, always perseveres. Love never fails.
(1 Corinthians 13:7-8)

Kris became sick about four months after we got married. It was unexpected and disabling and is now in its sixth year. This is not the way I envisioned our marriage. This sort of thing shouldn't happen to a young man in the prime of his life. And it shouldn't happen to love. That's been one of the lessons of his illness—that it was sent by the enemy to steal away Kris' life and to crush us. It was sent to make love fail.

But a funny thing happened on the way to robbing, killing and destroying—God showed up! I have to admit, I have wished for Him to show up differently from time to time. Of course, my desire is that God would have healed Kris immediately and completely. But He didn't, perhaps in part because our understanding of healing was so incomplete. The good that God has brought into the situation includes our lessons in perseverance. I learned in a new and fresh way that love involves sacrifice. Kris learned he was worth more than his performance and his ability to work.

I've been reminded again and again of the viciousness of the enemy and of his commitment to wreaking havoc. But mostly, I've been reminded that love, born of God, does not fail. It is not weak.

Rather, it is purified and strengthened by the fire. Costly though that is, I am grateful for the chance to see love vindicated.

Father, we invite You to shake in us what can be shaken, that what remains would be unshakable. Lord, purify our love. Let it indeed be patient and kind, full of hope and mercy, and a balm for the things that ail us. Amen.

In Sickness and in Love

Myrna Pugh

The two will become one flesh. (Ephesians 5:31)

I have always known that my husband, Pat, loved and cherished me. That has never been in question. But I never knew just how much Pat loved me until recently. A few months ago a lifelong chronic illness turned deadly as a devastating infection threatened to take my life. My body was weak and depleted, and my immune system had collapsed. I lay in bed one long night, exhausted and ready to give up. Pat sat beside me, not sure if I would survive the night. I awoke from a half-sleeping state to the sound of someone weeping and praying softly. I heard my husband fervently pleading with God to spare my life.

I listened in wonder, not because I didn't know Pat loved me that much, but because I didn't know that *he* knew that he loved me that much. I heard a plea that I am sure he had never uttered before—a plea for me to remain with him

Listening to Pat's powerful prayers for me, something turned over inside me. I felt my soul being knit to his, and I knew that God had answered his prayers for me. I knew for certain that I would live. I can't tell you how I knew this; I simply knew it.

After nearly thirty years of marriage, I felt the bonding that many couples never feel. I felt more loved and cared for than at any other time in our marriage. My heart swelled within me, and I too began to pray for myself.

Months later, I am recovering from my ordeal. I probably will always have to deal with this problem, but something wonderful has changed. My husband and I are closer to one another and to God than ever before. Pat is more real and open with me. He prays with a new fervency.

I too am changed from my experience. I tell Pat often how much I love him and how much I appreciate his love. I can feel his careful attention toward me, and I love it.

In "sickness and in health" means much more today than it did so many years ago. Sometimes "sickness" can be the most "healthy" place to be if God is present, because He can change us there.

Dear Lord, thank You that You are the One who truly heals us from the inside out. Help us to allow You to enter into our pain, sicknesses and hurts and bring the relief that only You can give. Walk along beside us in our suffering today, Father. Thank You for who You are. Amen.

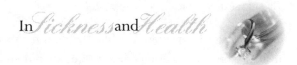

The Way He Loves

Nancy Hagerman

*Husbands, love your wives, just as Christ loved the church and gave
himself up for her.* (Ephesians 5:25)

One day in September 1996 I completely broke down. My brain
would not work. I couldn't remember my name. Tears flowed as
I tried to get dressed, because the decision of what to wear was
too much. Worse was the all-encompassing panic. My mouth
felt dry and I began hyperventilating. Uncontrollable screams
rose from deep inside. I felt as though I might start running
wildly through the streets, tearing my hair and shrieking.

A friend drove me to the hospital. It seemed an eternity as I
waited in the emergency room. Remaining still was impossible. I
paced continually, wringing my hands or swinging my arms in
wide arcs. The doctor spent only a few minutes with me before
he sent me upstairs to the psych ward.

A few weeks later when my husband obtained a pass to take
me out of the hospital for dinner, I was as nervous as a teenager
on a first date. He had promised to care for me "in sickness and
health," but neither of us had considered mental illness. I was
plagued by uncontrollable mood swings, ranging from clinging
and dependent to abusive and hostile in a matter of hours.

Does he truly love me or merely feel sorry for me? I wondered. *Will he
decide to remain with me out of pity? Or leave because life is too unpleas-*

ant around me? I considered telling the doctor I wouldn't see my husband, but the meeting couldn't be postponed forever. I was waiting when he arrived.

What can be better than finding out someone loves you for who you are rather than for what you do? The mental breakdown didn't matter to my husband. Although he confesses he turned to the Lord often in the days of my illness, not knowing how much more he could take, he loved me and was committed to staying by my side for the rest of my life. Remembering his promise at our wedding, he chose to remain faithful. How could I not get well with support like that?

At present we have been married for almost twenty-nine years. Bipolar illness is a battle for both one's mind and life against the powers of darkness. Though I still struggle at times, Jesus has taught me a number of things about spiritual warfare, and with my husband's love sustaining me, I continue to remain stable. He is a hero to me today and a living example of Christ's love for His Bride, the Church.

> *Father, sometimes we don't feel like loving each other. Help us remember to keep our eyes on You—to learn to love one another through the way that You love us. Amen.*

[Excerpted from *In the Pit: A Testimony of God's Faithfulness to a Bipolar Christian,* © 2001 by Nancy Hagerman. Published by Essence Publishing.]

The Missing Clue

Jean R. Mays

The LORD will guide you always. (Isaiah 58:11)

As I eased into the shadowy parking space at the senior center, a glow in the sky caught my eye. Straight ahead, under a cloudless blue sky, a golden light shimmered over the towering Sandia Mountains framing East Albuquerque. I watched in wonder as the browns of the massive sentinels changed to a bright pink-purple.

It was as if an unseen hand had funneled the late afternoon oranges, reds and golds through a moving searchlight just for me, just for that moment. I *knew* the Lord was spelling out h-o-p-e. Hope that there was an answer for the guilt that had been weighing me down for months as the reality I kept trying to deny was fast approaching. I was going to have to move my Alzheimer's-crippled husband into a nursing home.

Perhaps this was the evening when I would get the clue I needed from one of the fifty family members at our Alzheimer's support group meeting—the clue that would show me how to ease Ray's transition from his favorite desk to a strange one.

He hadn't even bothered to look up from his desk as his sitters said a cheery hello. I gave him a good-bye peck on the cheek, but he was too busy to acknowledge me—too preoccupied with his "work" of rearranging paper clips according to size and lining up containers of red, green, blue and black pencil leads like soldiers. He had used these same lead pencils to map sketches of the moon for the astronauts' first landing—a NASA-assigned project for his engineering team.

Entering the senior center, I took my seat among that sea of blank faces . . . a room of lost hope. Shipwrecked. All of them, like me, struggling to care for a loved one whose message systems, like so many sets of tiny Christmas lights, were beginning to dim, perhaps blink, perhaps brighten again or perhaps go out for good, as my neurologist had explained to me in his kind "kindergarten" tone.

Tonight, rather than a program of medical or legal gobbledygook, was simply to be a sharing session. As I munched on a cookie, a happy voice grabbed my attention.

"I worried all afternoon that he'd be furious with me for leaving him at the day care center. But I could hardly believe it . . . the director said he had a *wonderful* time with the others! He was busy every minute playing checkers, helping steer a wheelchair and reading the newspaper to three attentive residents. And guess what? Several days later, he came to me and said, 'Marie, when am I going back to the club?' "

Club! That was it! I'd found the missing clue! Our lives together had included military clubs everywhere. Swimming, tennis, golf . . . Good friends . . . *Good memories!*

Weeks later Ray was hospitalized for a suspected tumor. Although it was visible on the X-rays, the doctors were unable to locate it—another miracle! When Ray arrived at the nursing facility via ambulance, I said, "You'll enjoy the *club* while you recuperate from these tests."

It worked! Ray often commented, "I'm sure the tennis courts are on the other side of the fence."

Thank You, Lord, for being with Ray and me in sickness and health and for the assurance that one day we will again be together on the other side of the fence. Amen.

PART FIVE

Forsaking All Others

A One-Way Aisle

Kathleen Hayes

Let marriage be held in honor among all, and let the marriage bed be undefiled; for God will judge the immoral and adulterous. . . . Be content with what you have; for he has said, "I will never fail you nor forsake you." (Hebrews 13:4-5, RSV)

I woke up in the middle of the night, my heart pounding. I had just been dreaming about an old boyfriend. Again. I rolled over, determined to get him out of my mind, and put my arm around my husband, who snuggled up against me as he slept. *Please, Lord, help me to dream about my husband, not others.*

I know that God does not condemn me for such dreams, but I believe I am suffering the consequences of many years of less- than-godly dating. Although technically I kept myself pure, I stayed in some unhealthy relationships way too long, sometimes dated two men at once and dated a few non-Christians. These unhealthy patterns were deeply ingrained in me by the time I met the wonderful man who would become my husband.

After walking down that one-way aisle at age forty-one, I encountered the normal adjustments and challenges of married life. Lifelong faithfulness with no escape clause was scary! Sometimes I wanted to "break up" and find someone else. Emotionally I had not fully forsaken all others, although I had pledged to do so on my wedding day.

It's no accident that the familiar promise, "I will never leave you or forsake you" (see Hebrews 13:5), comes right after some strong words against marital infidelity. Jesus does not abandon us, and we are not to forsake our marriage partners through adultery or fornication, in thought or in action. We are to be content with what we have.

As a wife, I needed to change my "dating mentality" into a "marriage mentality." I confessed my sinful thoughts to the Lord, my husband and a few friends who agreed to pray for me. I asked God to help me be content in marriage. As God answers that prayer, I am learning to forsake all others and devote myself to my husband alone, and we are growing in intimacy and joy. In the same way, as we forsake all other gods and devote ourselves fully to Jesus Christ, we can experience the joy of growing closer and closer to Him.

Lord, You know our sinful tendencies and yet promise to never forsake us. We refuse to nurture these tendencies but surrender them to You. Help us to be content, Lord, and to forsake all others so that You will be glorified in our lives. Amen.

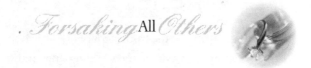

Escaping the Riptide

Jane Moran

One night as I lay in bed, I yearned deeply for my lover, but he did not come. So I said to myself, "I will get up now and roam the city, searching for him in all its streets and squares." But my search was in vain.
(Song of Songs 3:1–2, NLT)

Those who live along the coast of North Carolina often hear about the dangers of riptides—strong currents of water that form when the wind is blowing hard from the beach out to sea. They can whisk an unsuspecting swimmer out to sea very quickly. While many are rescued, many drown before help can reach them.

Sometimes it seems like life is a series of riptides; you can be living a leisurely life and suddenly be sucked into a strong current of activity that threatens to drown you.

When I was single, I never questioned the hectic pace of my life. At one point, I was working full-time, attending graduate school and helping lead two large singles groups. I'd like to say that when I married I instantly reordered my life to give priority to my marriage, but I can't. I continued to accept new responsibilities and ministry opportunities. Tony and I did much of the ministry "together," but, of course, time spent in large groups isn't really "time together." At one point, I was out of the house almost every night!

When Tony challenged me one night about the effects of some of my "time habits," I became furious. "How *dare* he try to control me!" I fumed, sitting on the front steps of our little house. I remember removing my engagement and wedding rings and studying them in the streetlight. At that moment, they seemed more like handcuffs than tokens of commitment.

As I looked at them, the phrase "time adultery" floated across my mind. I recognized that allowing myself to be drawn away into activities—even worthwhile activities—was essentially committing adultery. It was taking time that rightfully belonged to my husband and giving it to others.

As the conviction sank in, I was reminded of riptides. Swimmers can be happily swimming one moment and suddenly be sucked out to sea the next because of a single misstep. They can escape if they recognize the problem and swim parallel to shore until they swim out of the riptide; but if they do not take action, they can easily drown.

I don't want to drown my marriage in the riptide of time adultery. Managing my time is a constant balancing act, but an incredibly worthwhile one.

Lord, help me to recognize the currents that run through my life and draw me away from prioritizing time with my spouse. Help me to swim parallel to the shores of Your purposes when I become busy and to value my marriage above any other ministry. Amen.

"You're Sending Us Where, Lord?"

Marty Cottrill

Don't be afraid, for I am with you. (Isaiah 41:10, NLT)

"Turkey?! Where's that? I thought we'd be going to England or Germany," I said in response to my husband's bad news that his next assignment as an Air Force chaplain would take us to Ankara, Turkey.

"It will be a great experience," said Dave with his typical enthusiasm. "Just think, we can even visit Ephesus!"

I knew of the early Christian community that had been started by the Apostle Paul, but I still had trouble seeing how I could cope with moving our family of four to this strange place.

For the next several weeks, I posted invisible DO NOT DISTURB signs on my life, trying to avoid the reality at hand. Meanwhile, Dave brought home booklets about Turkish customs and the American community in Ankara, as well as guidance regarding what to take with us. We applied for passports, endured vaccinations and made difficult decisions about what to take and what to store. I cried. I poured my feelings into my journal and cried some more. I still desperately wanted the assignment to go away.

One Sunday evening, in the midst of a communion service, I was surprised to receive a personal bulletin about my dismal situation.

My husband's message to the small congregation included an invitation to ask Jesus how we could love and serve Him better. Though I wanted to do my loving and serving right where I was, I immediately saw a large chalkboard in front of me with a simple list that I couldn't miss:

1. Be willing to follow.
2. Be willing to let go.
3. Trust Me to be with you.

Quite unexpectedly, Dave's invitation to prayer became God's invitation to trust. To be willing to follow, I had to let go of several satisfying relationships and activities. Beyond that, I was being called to let go of my paralyzing fear of the unknown and trust God to guide our family through this new experience.

The chalkboard image sustained me as we said our good-byes and flew across the Atlantic. Through Dave's continued enthusiasm for the biblical riches of Asia Minor and the hospitable people we met there, God showed me that I could trust myself to Him. After all, Turkey was not "foreign territory" to Him.

Lord, help us trust You with our fears. When we face places or situations that are foreign to us, remind us that You are already there, welcoming us and inviting us to grow. And help us, as spouses, to encourage each other in our lifelong journeys in faith. Amen.

God's Ways Are Always Best

Marita Littauer

You wives, submit yourselves to your husbands, for that is what the Lord has planned for you. (Colossians 3:18, TLB)

The nature of a crisis is that when it is yours, it is huge. You can logically measure your problem with someone else's and realize that you do not have it so bad. But that only lasts so long. As soon as your situation hits you in the face, you are overwhelmed again.

For months I had been wrestling in my spirit over a crisis that appeared to have no solution. Due to upheaval in his industry, my husband had been forced to seek employment out-of-state. The problem was, I did not want to leave New Mexico, and so I kept beating both of us up. I wasn't at all pleasant.

Finally I was able to look at what I saw to be the obstacles. One of my biggest hangups was my business. Personally, I actually like to move, but my business was established. It had been supporting us during this difficult time. I had great employees and I loved my work. I couldn't just up and move!

Once I faced my fears, I knew I needed to stop and ask God what He wanted for my life. It didn't take a theologian to figure out God's priority. Put my business first or my marriage first? Hmmm . . . If I believed in the Bible, if I believed in God's Word—which I did and still do—I knew I had to put my marriage first. In this case, it meant accepting a move. If God gave me this business, which I believed He had, He would take care of it.

The amazing thing is that the moment I reached that place, my sense of crisis lifted and I was at total peace. I told my employees, who are all Christians too, that I would be commuting between New Mexico and Colorado. They applauded my decision.

My husband accepted the position. I got him settled and decorated his temporary home. I cooked him dinners and left him prepared meals in the freezer. Together we made the best of a difficult situation. For a while, we lived in two states with me, my dog, our main house and the business in one state and my husband, his job, his dog and his apartment in the next. I made the five-and-a-half-hour trek between states on the weekends when I was not on the road speaking.

This commuter marriage lasted for six months. We are now back in the same state, and God has blessed my actions. Chuck has his pick of job opportunities in New Mexico. And our marriage is stronger than ever!

Help me always to put my marriage first and to submit to my husband's needs. Thank You that Your ways are always best! Amen.

[Excerpted and edited from *You've Got What It Takes: Celebrating Being a Woman Today,* © 2000 Marita Littauer. Published by Bethany House Publishers.]

Looking for Better Opportunities

Chuck Noon

Live happily with the woman you love through the fleeting days of life,
for the wife God gives you is your best reward down here for all your
earthly toil. (Ecclesiastes 9:9, TLB)

For men, it's human nature to identify ourselves with our jobs and careers. Our self-esteem is based upon what we do, our job titles. The world daily reinforces this with emphasis on self, status and the acquisition of personal net worth.

God's model is the opposite. He emphasizes treasure in heaven and dedication to our wives here on earth. "Husbands, love your wives, just as Christ loved the church and gave himself up for her" (Ephesians 5:25).

Marita has followed me in several moves as I have pursued success. While I always had a job, I couldn't quite get ahead. Believing that better opportunities awaited me in Colorado, I became licensed there, took a job and rented a small apartment.

Marita made the best of it, but it was very hard on her. She couldn't easily move. She has great employees and wonderful friends and is very happy in Albuquerque. Yet she drove back and forth between Albuquerque and Colorado Springs—five and a half hours—almost every weekend. She was stressed and exhausted and had three automobile accidents during those six months.

One evening while I was out walking my dog, Harley, in the snow, wishing he would hurry up and do his thing, God spoke to me. Now, God has only spoken to me three or four times in my life in a clearly audible voice. So when He does, I listen. God told me, "Go home and take care of your wife." This was not what I wanted to hear, as God's direction seldom is. I thought, *If I'm going to do this, I really ought to be in the same state.* I obeyed and moved back to New Mexico. I took a job that I considered to be way beneath my abilities and education. For a year and a half I worked in that humble position. During that time, I read the Bible through cover-to-cover, and God went to work where He couldn't before. I didn't look for a better job, but God selected one for me.

Once I put my wife first—not my career or my search for success—I was offered a job in my field that was impressive and paid more than I had ever made before. Since that time, I have been offered many other positions and have my pick of opportunities. When I was seeking success and my own interests, success eluded me. When I was willing to do what was best for my marriage (basically love Marita extravagantly), I found the success I worked so hard to find.

While God's way doesn't seem to make sense to the world, it is the best way.

> *Lord, help me make Your priorities my priorities. I desire Your best for my marriage, for my job, for my life. Amen.*

A Holy Jealousy

Wanda G. Schwandt

Put me like a seal over your heart, like a seal on your arm. For love is as strong as death, jealousy is as severe as Sheol; its flashes are flashes of fire, the very flame of the LORD. (Song of Solomon 8:6, NASB)

From across the room I witnessed her touching his arm, her coy giggle and intense eye contact. The nerve of that woman, advancing on my husband while we were guests in her home! Feigning illness, I made our apologies.

During the ride home, I boiled with irritation. "Weren't you aware of what she was doing?" I asked Mark.

"What are you worried about? Through sixteen years of marriage, haven't I proven my faithfulness to you? You are the only woman I love," he responded.

He was right! I wondered why the woman's futile efforts had bothered me so much instead of raising a calm assurance. Silently I asked the Lord to show me the reason for my insecurity.

Over the years our love has grown and changed. As young lovers, we had no trouble forsaking others. The fire of our love for one another burned intensely. Over time, our love deepened into glowing coals, fed with the fuel of uninterrupted time, deep communication and an abundance of small gestures. But then daily responsibilities and family needs began to take precedence over our relationship.

Confronted with the threat this woman posed, I realized that I had taken my husband for granted. I was jealous for his faithfulness and devotion to me alone.

Without perpetual feeding, marriages cool and die out. King Solomon's wife recognized the intense heat of jealousy and asked to be branded onto her husband's heart and arm, like an ever-present tattoo, as a sign of mutual devotion.

I'm grateful that my jealousy alerted me to what is missing in our relationship. Now we plan seasonal weekend getaways, e-mail sweet nothings during the day and chat face-to-face each night before bed to keep the home fires burning. We put our relationship before all others except our devotion to God.

Lord, we desire to keep the passionate fire of love burning within our marriage and toward You. Guard us against temptation and show us many ways that we can deepen our connection with You and each other every day. Amen.

Marriage Is . . .

the union of two spirits,

the bonding of best friends

on the deepest level,

saying "ours" instead of "mine"

and "we" instead of "I"

and loving the sound of it.

—J. L. Hardesty

Ho Ho Ho and
a Bottle of Aspirin
Lynn Ward

No city or house divided against itself will last or continue to stand.
(Matthew 12:25, AMP)

As newlyweds, my husband and I lived those first few months on love and occasional trips to Acme Supermarket. I reveled in the anticipation of sharing Christmas, my absolutely-can't-possibly-be-beat favorite time of the year, with the love of my life.

We're lucky we didn't celebrate the joyful day with a double murder!

Looking back, I can see that the problem was obvious to anyone not visually impaired by love. In theory, we celebrated the same holiday; in practical fact, our traditions couldn't have been more different.

I started shopping in October. He wanted to know why I was rushing. I got out the decorations (purchased so frugally the year before at a seventy-five-percent-off sale) the day after Thanksgiving. He thought I was nuts.

Then the week before Christmas, when I announced that I was ready to go buy the tree, he stared at me as though I had suddenly turned into a Keebler elf.

Our fiercest battle was over whether to have an angel or a star on the top of the tree. We ended up with a generic sort of bauble for the first few years because I couldn't find a five-pointed star like the one I was used to. Eventually we did buy an angel, but only because years of not finding a proper star had worn me down. I'd like to report that I acquiesced gracefully, but I don't like to lie.

You may be wondering, didn't I notice before we were married that his family had different Christmas traditions than mine? Of course I did. I'm not dumb! During the three years we dated, I participated in many of their holiday activities. But it honestly never occurred to me that our first Christmas would be a problem. After all, my family's traditions were so obviously better—no, so obviously *right*—that it never crossed my mind that my husband wouldn't embrace all of my ideas with complete abandon.

I think I got through that first holiday season on enthusiasm alone. For the next several years I continued to believe that he would "see the light." At long last, we started to work out our own traditions, and in this spirit of compromise . . .

"No. No, wait! The wise men always go to the right of the manger."

Where did I put that aspirin?

Heavenly Father, help us to give up our own wants so that we can build a strong marriage based on Your plan for us. We want our union to be a blessing to each other and an example of Your love to others. In Jesus' name, Amen.

Marriage is respecting, even enjoying,

one another's differences.

–J.L. Hardesty

A Different Kind of Love Story

Linda S. Lee

For if you forgive men their trespasses, your heavenly Father will also forgive you. But if you do not forgive men their trespasses, neither will your Father forgive your trespasses. (Matthew 6:14-15, NKJV)

One Valentine's Day I returned home to a note and a luxury perfume box on the master bed. The note read, "I can't live with you anymore. I want to die—Terry." I bawled and screamed, but overcame the urge to hurl the perfume through my bay window. Terry returned, but we lost any pretense of intimacy. He soon left again for good, saying he'd nearly killed himself with a friend's gun before he had gone the last time. He moved to our sailboat to work through his problems with the help of a Christian counselor.

When he asked for a divorce after three months of separation, we had been married for twenty-three years. We had two barely grown sons and a seven-year-old daughter. Terry said that he had loved another woman the year before. They had engaged in an affair for months. His depression began after she refused to be intimate with him while he was married.

"I don't think I ever loved you," Terry said. I didn't believe him, but I felt helpless to change his mind. I agreed to give him a divorce and made plans to leave the area. I believe my plans to leave allowed Terry the freedom to decide what he wanted. He eventually chose me, in part because he could not justify divorcing me to marry his lover.

When he asked me to take him back and rebuild our marriage, I didn't think I could forgive him or trust him again. But according to Scripture, I saw that I had no choice. I had to forgive if I wanted God's forgiveness for my own sins. That didn't mean I had to accept Terry back into the marriage; nevertheless, I felt God telling me I could trust Him to care for me if we reconciled.

I had stiff requirements about accountability, counseling and absolutely no contact with the former lover. Terry agreed to each requirement before he moved home.

We learned to communicate in an understanding way, without blame or attack. Terry dealt with guilt, depression and moral accountability. It took time for him to get over loving the other woman. I hated that part, but we faced truth head-on.

First I learned how to heal from my anger habit, where I flew into rages and then blamed others for them. Then I learned about forgiveness. Mostly I learned that there were no innocent partners in our marriage disaster. We worked on forgiving one another. It was the hardest work we have ever done, but the most rewarding.

In time we were set free—Terry from adultery and depression, and me from rage and control. We are free to love again. We can still be tempted, but we recognize our limits and trust God to forgive our sins as we confess them. We are content to love each other until death.

Ten years later our children say they learned important lessons about love and forgiveness from us. Terry and I are better off and much happier than we were before our crisis. But I don't recommend our path. Any couple can learn forgiveness and loving communication without the pain we incurred.

Father, thank You for forgiving our sins. Thank You for healing our marriage and giving us life and joy in place of death and rage. Nothing is too great for You. We rejoice in Your power. Hallelujah! Amen.

But He Never Lifts a Finger!

Susan Kimmel Wright

Hope in God, who richly provides us with everything for our enjoyment. (1 Timothy 6:17)

By the time my mother-in-law arrived, I was sick with exhaustion. For two months I'd been on twenty-four-hour duty, caring for adopted, newborn twin daughters. My husband and son had come to Honduras to initiate the adoption proceedings but had returned to the United States after a few weeks.

Even when my husband had been there, I'd struggled alone to care for all three children. Again and again I'd dragged myself out of bed at night to answer wailing cries. Alone I'd boiled water, mixed formula, changed diapers and washed out clothing in the bathroom sink.

Now my mother-in-law was here with a package of "goodies" from home, including some books by my favorite author for those long, wakeful nights. "I just want you to know what a good husband you have," she told me. "He went all over town looking for these. I hope you appreciate it."

My loneliness and fatigue exploded into anger. "Did he tell you how he never lifted a finger to help with the kids? And when I mentioned how tired I am, he said all I do is complain!"

My mother-in-law took the babies so I could sit down and relax. She said soothing things, and soon I felt good enough to look past my weariness.

I remembered how Dave had run all over Tegucigalpa, untangling red tape so that we could adopt the second, unexpected baby and bring her home. He wasn't "Mr. Mom" by a long shot, and in an earlier century I probably wouldn't have expected him to be. But he helped in many other ways, including running all those errands I find so exhausting.

When we marry, we may vow lightly to forsake all others, thinking it unlikely we'll be tempted into an illicit relationship. But far more seductive than the allure of an attractive stranger is the fairytale myth that we're entitled to an ideal spouse. We don't really want to forget that long-dreamed-of Prince Charming who will meet all our needs.

No human being can ever meet another's every need, and most—myself included—fall woefully short in more than one area. God never intended that we find our fulfillment in another person, but only in Himself. His grace alone is sufficient for us, and only He can supply our every need.

Just a cup of coffee and ten minutes in the rocking chair enabled me to stop comparing Dave to the gilt-edged picture of "Mr. Right" I'd been carrying in my heart. When I did, I could appreciate the very human husband God had given me and the many blessings he's brought into my life.

Precious Lord, how grateful I am that I have only to look to You and Your limitless provision for what I need in life. Make me more grateful today for the blessing of my spouse, and help me in turn be a spouse who responds to my partner's needs. Amen.

Becoming One
After Being One

Jane Moran

If you try to keep your life for yourself, you will lose it. But if you give up your life for me, you will find true life. (Matthew 16:25, NLT)

When I finally became engaged I felt more than ready to marry. I had held countless bridal showers for friends, served football fields of wedding cake and poured oceans of punch. I had smiled and waved friends off on their honeymoons through showers of birdseed. Privately I would mourn what I knew would be the distancing of a friend as she joined the "married" world. But now it was finally my turn! Yet as I prepared for my wedding, married friends pulled me aside. "You've been single a long time," they cautioned. "It's going to be a hard adjustment."

I listened solemnly and steeled myself for what I knew would be a turbulent time.

After our wedding, I came home and waited for Tony to sprout fangs. I watched for annoying habits to emerge, but none did. We soon discovered that neither of us cared where the toothpaste was squeezed, how the toilet tissue was hung or where the dishrag ended up. Many would call us blessed, and we are.

But that is not to say my adjustment was effortless. I had prepared myself for a boxing match, not a bobsled race. I had expected conflict and arguments, but instead I discovered that I was more unsettled by the need to adjust the rhythm of my life to another person's. Our first fight occurred when I simply forgot that there was someone at home who not only cared when I got there, but worried when I was late. There was an unsettling loss of privacy, and even my devotional life was disrupted. My free time seemed to evaporate as I became more conscious about things like meal planning and housekeeping.

But perhaps the most disconcerting thing about marriage was realizing that Tony needed to set our direction, not me. I knew that if I didn't allow Tony to lead, our marriage would be off balance and our "bobsled" would be destined to crash. It was hard to trust someone else to "steer," but God reminded me that I had done precisely that when I had surrendered my life to Him. Ironically, the years before I became a Christian, when I was "in control of my own destiny," were some of the most miserable of my life. It wasn't until I "lost" my life to Christ that I gained it. My marriage was also a "loss" which has added more to my life than I could have ever imagined. I am grateful that I took the chance to "lose my life."

Lord, thank You for turning what the world perceives as loss into heavenly gain. Help us not to see the adjustments required by marriage as loss but rather as an investment that will yield eternal benefits. Amen.

Three's a Crowd

Marilynn Griffith

He said, "What have they seen in your house?" So Hezekiah answered, "They have seen all that is in my house; there is nothing among my treasuries that I have not shown them." (2 Kings 20:15, NASB)

"Who are you talking to, honey?" my husband, home early from work, asked as he slipped up behind me.

Still laughing, I twisted in my seat and kissed him on the cheek. "Melissa. I'm telling her about that time you made the Christmas tree out of tomato wire. Do we still have those pictures?"

"Somewhere. Maybe in the garage."

I didn't notice it, but my husband's voice faded then. After eight years of marriage, I never realized how often I hurt him by sharing private things to people outside our family.

I giggled and told a few more tales before I realized he was gone. "I'd better go, Melissa. I'll talk to you later."

I found my husband in the closet, positioning his boots behind the door so the babies couldn't get them. His smile was noticeably absent, but he didn't say a word.

"Are you mad at me?"

He sighed. "No."

I rolled my eyes. Here we go again. I knew he was mad, but getting information out of my husband is like watching a plant grow—if you've got enough patience, eventually you'll get something. Patience isn't my strong suit. I have the tribulations to prove it.

"Just say it, OK? I'm sorry about the kitchen. . . ."

"It isn't that. It's the way you always . . ."

My hands shifted to my hips and my eyes narrowed to slits. "What?" I asked in a tone louder than necessary.

"Talk about me. About the kids. About everybody. You think we're all material for your personal comedy show."

I opened my mouth to respond and shut it again. He was right. I came from a family of people who constantly poked fun at each other with anyone who would listen. I hated it as a child and vowed I would never do it. Yet here I was doing it anyway.

Now, looking into my husband's eyes, guilt washed over me. I had hurt my partner, my best friend. I buried myself in my husband's chest and begged his forgiveness, cringing at the thought of stories I'd told about him at baby showers and women's retreats. Instead of telling people how creative and wonderful he was, I'd been revealing my husband's inner self, his treasure, to people it didn't belong to.

Two years later, I still slip up and share things that I shouldn't. My husband even joins in sometimes and finishes the story. However, the more time I invest in making my marriage the priority relationship, the fewer precious jewels pass my lips.

Lord, forgive us for allowing people to rummage through our marriages, viewing things that should be for our eyes only. Help us to remember that our spouses are sacred treasures. Restore the intimacy and trust lost through careless words and actions. Amen.

Just Say No

Gail Black Kopf

There is a time for everything, and a season for every activity under heaven. (Ecclesiastes 3:1)

The eerie glow of the television screen was all that greeted me as I entered our living room. My husband sulked on the couch. The remains of his TV dinner sat on the coffee table. Once again a crushing guilt flooded me.

"Why is it that you're always so busy helping other people with their problems that I have to come home to an empty house?" he demanded.

"But Cleo doesn't drive," I said. "How else is she going to get to the VA hospital in Richmond to see her husband?"

A wall of silence separated us as we got ready for bed. Throughout our twenty-year marriage I'd often heard the same accusation from Mike. I wanted to practice the Golden Rule. He countered with "Charity begins at home." Lately his complaints had become more frequent, and I sensed that it was just a matter of time before the issue came to a head.

With the Holy Spirit's nudging, it slowly dawned on me that Mike's objections were the symptoms of a deeper problem. My husband needed to know that he was a priority in my life—that I was committed to him and our marriage more than I was to the host of "worthy causes" that clamored for my attention.

Had I overextended myself? As the classic child of an alcoholic, I've always had a hard time saying "no." I envied Eve, who didn't have earthly parents, in-laws, a host of relatives and friends who invaded the Garden of Eden at the drop of a fig leaf, or a church congregation that demanded huge segments of her time. Yet her marriage wasn't perfect. Like me, Eve had a hard time saying "no."

Part of the solution was obvious: I needed to downsize. I began to cancel and rearrange my activities so that when Mike came home from work I was there to greet him. Even if it was just fast food, we had dinner together as a family and a "snuggle time" afterwards.

When Mike became enamored with our new computer, it was apparent that we both needed to balance the responsibilities in our marriage. Traveling the information superhighway, he'd be lost in cyberspace for hours. I hoped the initial excitement would wear off, but it didn't. Yard work and chores went undone as Mike escaped after dinner and on weekends to an on-line service or one of the video games he'd installed.

"This time," I gently reminded him, "it's your turn to just say no."

Lord, give me discernment so I can say "no" to the world and "yes" to You. Only then can I glorify You through my marriage. Amen.

"But Honey, I Was
Only Teasing!"
Miggy Krentel

Man looks at the outward appearance, but the LORD looks at the heart. (1 Samuel 16:7, NASB)

"Who drove you home from choir tonight, Miggy?" my husband asked. Suddenly the room had grown warmer.

"Bill." I felt my cheeks flush. "You know him. . . ."

Stationed at the naval proving grounds in Virginia, Paul and I felt blessed to be living together when so many couples were apart during the war.

"Do you have choir practice every Thursday?" Paul continued to stand there.

Choosing not to answer made me drop the pile of catalogs I was carrying to the trash. Paul looked at me. He was clearly puzzled at my behavior.

"Miggy, sometimes you make me think that there's some flirting going on here."

What had I done to provoke this statement? Bill was kind of handsome, but hey, Paul and I had just celebrated our tenth anniversary.

"Listen, honey," Paul said, smiling lovingly, "I know you would never cheat on me, but the way you kid around and always manage to sit next to him makes me very uncomfortable."

I squirmed. Knowing deep inside that what my husband said was a good description of my actions, I felt guilty. Paul kept right on "preaching": "It's just that Bill might misinterpret your actions."

I knew what he meant. I turned and walked out of the room, leaving the catalogs behind in a messy pile.

By our bed was an open Bible. I looked away. I didn't feel like a lecture from God right now. Instead I picked up the *New York Times* and started scanning it. One sentence caught my eye: "Linda appeared to be involved with her local banker, often seen riding with him in his car."

Clearly God speaks to us through many channels! I swallowed hard and began to pray.

Dear God, I know what You are thinking. I guess I thought it was all safe, shallow waters. But I know in my heart it has the appearance of something more. But God, You and I know there is nothing. I love my Paul. Please help me show him. Amen.

Date Night

Candy Abbott

"For whom am I toiling," he asked, "and why am I depriving myself of enjoyment?" (Ecclesiastes 4:8)

"Where are we going tonight?" I chirped with a smile as I walked through the door.

"I don't know," Drew answered. "What do you feel like?"

It was Friday, and this was our typical "Honey, I'm home" greeting. For twenty-six years we've had a rock-solid marriage that people admire, and I credit our "Date Night" as one of the reasons.

I still remember the conversation that triggered our decision to forsake all others for a few hours each week. We were on our honeymoon.

"Sounds good," Drew said. "But when? Any time we get a chance to break away? Or a specific night?"

"I think we need to be consistent. If we try to grab a 'date' whenever we can, it's likely not to happen at all. Do you prefer Friday or Saturday night?"

"Let's claim Fridays." Drew beamed at the prospect. "After working hard all week, it'll do us good to get away."

Date Night didn't just happen. We've had to work at it by teaching our children, friends and relatives to respect our Friday nights. Hmmm, let's see—twenty-six years, fifty-two Fridays a year . . . Gosh, that's 1,352 dates we guarded! People often preface their invitations with "I know it's your date night, but. . . ." (We make exceptions for special occasions.)

Where do we go and what do we do on our dates? Most often it's a leisurely dinner out and back home around 9. Sometimes we'll decide where we're going a few days ahead of time, but most often we'll be in the car, pulling out of the driveway, before we know where we're headed. Restaurants we've tried range from hot dog stands to gourmet food—sometimes close to home, sometimes an hour's drive away. To guard against predictability, we might explore off-the-beaten-path places, walk on the beach, play tennis, stroll around the block, see a movie or go window-shopping. Usually when we think we're too busy for "alone time," that's when we need it most.

A funny thing happens when couples take time to gaze into each other's eyes. They talk about things that might otherwise be lost in the shuffle—small happenings, big dreams, tough problems, silly stuff, feelings—things that matter, things that don't. This together time (quiet talks, shared silences and candid moments) molds a marriage into what couples dream of when they say their vows.

God of love, help us not to be so distracted by our responsibilities that
we deprive ourselves of the pleasure of our spouses' company. Amen.

Team Spirit

Marilyn Yocum

So they are no longer two, but one. (Matthew 19:6)

"What? We're moving again?" I asked.

"It's up to you," my husband said. "If you don't want to, we'll stay and I'll look for another job around here."

I let out a big sigh. The company he worked for had been sold and the operation was moving 400 miles away. Many people were losing their jobs, but my husband had been offered a position with the new company if we were willing to move.

We were the lucky ones. I should have been glad. I should have been grateful. I should have jumped at the chance. Instead, all I could do was sigh.

We'd been transferred only once before, eight years earlier. It had taken almost all of those eight years for me to begin to feel like I fit in. Now the kids were no longer little, I had an eighteen-month-old business that was just beginning to take off and I was starting to make connections and get to know people.

"What are You doing to me, God?" I prayed. "I'm just beginning to build something of my own and now You're moving us?"

The next day, heavy laden, I dragged myself off to Wednesday morning Bible study at our church. I arrived early to set up the coffee and tea. My friend, Peggy, who is about ten years older than me, was early too.

"What's new with you?" she asked.

I told her the decision my husband and I were facing. "I've been wrestling with God all night," I said. "I know it's a good opportunity for my husband, but . . ."

"You're wondering when it's going to be your turn?"

"Yes! How did you know?"

"Oh, I know. We've moved four times, each time because of my husband's job. It seemed like every time I got settled, found a job I loved or got into a business of my own, it was time to up and move again."

"Four times? How did you manage?"

"All I can tell you is that God sees you as a team. It's impossible for Him to do something that is good for one of you and not good for the other one."

Her words helped clear the confusion in my mind. I began to see that the decision did not depend upon the outcome of a competition between my dreams and my husband's dreams. It depended on committing our future to God's plan for us. I stopped wrestling with God and asked just that He would show us the next step, the step for us to take as a team.

God, help me lay aside feelings of competition with my teammate, my spouse. Help me to remain committed to Your plan for us. Amen.

All That the Locusts
Have Eaten

Daniel Christian

*Be glad and rejoice. Surely the LORD has done great things. . . . The trees
are bearing their fruit; the fig tree and the vine yield their riches. "I will re-
pay you for the years the locusts have eaten."* (Joel 2:21-22, 25)

The May morning dawned, whispering the promise of an early
summer. The mellow glow of sunrise filled the room where my
wife and I both sat reading and praying.

It was time to admit to her that for twenty-three years a consum-
ing darkness had penetrated my life. It was time to confess that my
struggle to live with integrity was a war often lost. All that she
thought I was—a godly husband and leader—was based on a lie I
had learned to live well.

Promise Keepers shirts mocked me when I opened my
dresser drawer. I was not a promise keeper! The adversary convinced me that I was nothing more than a promise breaker.

Many say the affairs in my mind are harmless. Many claim this
is just the way "real men" are. But Jesus, the epitome of a "real
man," spoke against looking with lust upon a woman. Instead I
refused intimacy with my wife, clearly going against the biblical
mandate to enjoy the wife of my youth. For fifteen years she

longed for physical and emotional intimacy that I refused to offer. I was too wrapped up in the affairs in my mind.

The shock that gripped my wife's face that day as the gravity of my confession laid claim to her heart was overwhelming. However, I was drawn by the love of Christ and His promise to make me new in Him.

I stepped out of shame, admitted my guilt to my wife and prayed for her forgiveness and support. The burden began to lift. I sensed hope.

As we look back on the years since my confession, we see that God has exchanged the years the "locusts" had eaten at our marriage. Unsatisfied longings are now replaced by His sufficiency in a godly relationship with one another. We rejoice in knowing each other more than ever. Our love is deeper than we ever imagined. The fruit of our obedience blesses us daily. It began with my honest confession of a difficult truth and her willingness to forgive.

The adversary intended to destroy our marriage. God, however, delivered us from the infiltration of the evil of pornography. What began as an innocuous flirtation as a teenager mushroomed into addiction as an adult. But now it has been rendered impotent by the blood of Christ.

> *Oh Lord, we rejoice! We thank You that You repay for the years the locusts have eaten at our marriage. You provide fruitfulness and blessing out of that which the enemy intends for destruction. Lord, please give us courage to step out of shame and guilt into the fruitfulness that You provide. Thank You for Your promises made true in Christ. Amen.*

PART SIX

To Love and to Cherish

Beyond Love

Diana L. James

Let all bitterness, and wrath, and anger, and clamour, and evil speaking, be put away from you, with all malice: and be ye kind one to another, tenderhearted, forgiving one another, even as God for Christ's sake hath forgiven you. (Ephesians 4:31-32, KJV)

Just when I thought our seventeen-year marriage was humming along fairly smoothly, my husband jolted me today with the remark that I no longer treat him with honor and respect. I sat in stunned silence, trying to think what I had done that would make him say such a thing.

"It's not anything you've done," he explained. "It's just your attitude."

Although I didn't reply, my first thought was bitter and defensive: *Maybe you should work harder at earning my respect.* That ugly reaction was followed almost immediately by the humbling realization that Max was telling the truth—at least one side of it.

I swallowed hard and left the room. He followed me. I motioned to him that I wasn't ready to talk and I sure wasn't ready for a hug.

"Are you angry?" he asked.

"I need to do some processing," I replied, fighting back tears.

"I love you," he said softly.

"I need to do some processing," I said again in a wavering voice.

I got into the car and drove aimlessly around the neighborhood.

"Do you love me?" a starry-eyed bride-to-be asks her fiancé. The groom-to-be emphatically replies, "Of course I love you."

"Do you love me?" Tevye asks his wife of twenty years in the famous story *Fiddler on the Roof*.

Tevye's wife ponders her husband's question. She reminisces about all the meals she has cooked for him, all the clothes she has washed for him and the children she has given him over the years. After much thought, she replies, "Well, if that's love, I guess I love you."

Well then, what is love? Little kids "love" ice cream. Teenage boys "love" cars. Mom "loves" romantic movies, and Dad "loves" football games. The word depreciates with use. How can we talk about those kinds of love using the same word we use in songs like "Oh, How I Love Jesus" or "Jesus Loves Me"?

What the bride-to-be really wanted to know from her fiancé was not, "Do you love me as much as you love hot dogs and race cars?" No! She wanted reassurance that he cherished her in that moment and that he would cherish her forever.

As I drove around the neighborhood, the word *cherish* played itself over and over in my mind. When I finally came to an ah-ha! realization that the word *cherish* embodies the qualities of honor, esteem and respect, it was time for me to go home.

Max and I apologized to each other. We knelt in prayer again. We agreed to start over and from this day forward to really cherish one another with honor, esteem and respect.

It may take practice to cherish each other. I'm sure it will require an unselfish determination to go past the second mile—the mile beyond love.

Lord, help us to forgive each other, to be patient with each other, to bring out the best in one another and to seek Your guidance in using words and actions that convey honor, esteem and respect. Amen.

Love Extravagantly!

Marita Littauer

Observe how Christ loved us. His love was not cautious but extravagant.
He didn't love in order to get something from us but to give everything of
himself to us. Love like that. (Ephesians 5:2, *The Message*)

I was reading through Ephesians when God made one verse very clear to me. My personal mission, He told me, is to love my husband with extravagance—not to get, but to give everything of myself. As I cook breakfast or dinner, as I do the dishes, as I do the laundry—all of these things are something of myself I can give, not expecting to get in return.

Shortly after taking on this idea of loving extravagantly, I had to put it to the test. Chuck has a large model airplane that has been a part of his life for over twenty years. He built it and has too much of himself invested in it to risk flying it. With its five-foot wingspan, you cannot just tuck it anyplace. In our current home it hangs up near the peak of the cathedral ceiling in the family room. It is bright red with Red Baron-like decals. It is sure to be noticed. Since it is important to Chuck, I have accepted it as a conversation piece—and you can be sure it is!

Recently he took the airplane down to take it to a model airplane show. He spent hours cleaning off the accumulated dust that had firmly attached itself to every surface. The plane was very popular at the show, and he discovered how valuable it really is. Before he put it back on its hook, he wanted to protect it. He covered the body and wings with plastic dry cleaning bags, advertising and all.

I like my home to look like a showplace, so you can imagine that even having the airplane there is an act of compromise and love. Having it covered with baggy dry cleaning bags with words on them went too far. "I'll never be able to entertain again," I wailed. After my outburst, which I knew was an overreaction, I went outside and trimmed my roses. As I took a deep breath, "love extravagantly" came to mind. Does it really matter if the airplane has a bag over it? What is more important—that my husband be happy or that I have a lovely home? Hmmm . . . that was tough. *Love extravagantly*, I told myself.

I came back in and apologized, ready to accept the dry cleaning bags. Meanwhile, Chuck had decided that I was right and it was really ugly. He had taken the plane down, removed the dry cleaning bags and was replacing them with clear plastic wrap that didn't even show!

What changes do you need to make to love your spouse extravagantly? Make it your personal purpose statement. Love extravagantly!

> *Dear Lord, help me to make "love extravagantly" my personal mission statement. Remind me to love my spouse not cautiously but extravagantly—not to get, but to give! Amen.*

[Excerpted and edited from *Love Extravagantly: Making the Modern Marriage Work*, © 2001 Marita Littauer. Published by Bethany House Publishers.]

The Golf Shirts

Susan Petropulos

Now that I, your Lord and Teacher, have washed your feet, you also should wash one another's feet. (John 13:14)

My husband and I have been married for twenty-six years and that is just about how long we have argued about his golf shirts. The intimacy, friendship and support in marriage can be a blessing beyond compare. On the other side of the blessing are golf shirts!

Our basic problem was simple: I believe that ironing is optional. Wrinkles, it seems to me, are a natural part of life. I have them on my face; I have them on my body. And if wrinkles are OK for God, well, then wrinkles are OK for me. However, my husband does not see ironing the same way that I do. His mother ironed. She ironed her family's clothes; she ironed their sheets; she even ironed their underwear! From my husband's perspective, ironing is as necessary to civilized living as refrigeration, indoor plumbing and the telephone. To my husband, ironed golf shirts are not optional!

Why is it that we latch on to these little battles, ever sieging but never winning the war? I can't help but think that every married couple probably has something they can identify as a "golf shirt" problem. The problems are not serious enough to undermine the marriage or to threaten divorce, but when the row of golf shirts hanging in my laundry room replaces those available in my husband's closet, the battle cry goes out. The shirts are ironed, but my attitude does not change. I mutter and complain to God.

"Why is he so unreasonable, Lord? Can't he see that ironing golf shirts is a complete waste of my time?"

I never really expected an answer, but one day an answer came. I was once again grudgingly standing over a pile of "wrinkled" golf shirts, waiting for the iron to heat, when a crazy thought occurred to me: *Jesus is going to iron every one of these golf shirts.*

I looked around to be sure I was alone. There was no voice, no physical presence, but the thoughts in my head were definitely not my own. As I bent over the first shirt, I was reminded of Jesus on the night of the Last Supper. I saw Him kneeling down before each disciple, gently washing the dirt of the roadways from their feet, then drying them with a towel. Such a simple act of service. It really cost Him very little compared to the ultimate sacrifice which He was about to make.

Why is it so difficult for us to follow His example? Jesus Christ, the King of the universe, willingly served the people He loved. Whether it is emptying the ice cube trays, taking out the trash or ironing golf shirts, Jesus calls each one of us to sacrifice our way for someone else every day.

After twenty-six years the battle of the golf shirts is over. Now I see that ironing my husband's shirts is just one more way that I can show him that I love him. How many more wars in my life could come to an end if I would just start living like Jesus?

Oh Jesus, thank You for Your patience and Your grace. Please show me all the ways that I don't live like You. Please give me the power and the courage to change! Amen.

Loving Each Other

Cec Murphey

Love is patient and kind. Love is not jealous or boastful. (1 Corinthians 13:4, NLT)

When Shirley and I were dating, her mother made a statement that went something like this: "Some married people are kinder to their friends than they are to each other." Over the years I've thought about those words often and determined it wouldn't apply to us.

Sometimes, because we love each other, we tend to take the other for granted. We become more considerate of new relationships because we want to establish them. We already have loving relationships with our lovers and therefore do not show concern.

I've noticed that when many couples are in the dating stage, they're courteous and helpful. I've seen the dashing young fellow carefully open doors for the light of his life. I've often seen those same couples a year after their marriages. He gets out of the car and lets her get out by herself.

One of the things Shirley and I decided when we were dating was that I would continue opening doors for her all through our married life. I also said, "If I forget, I expect you to remind me." I'm still opening doors for Shirley because it's my way of saying I care about her and want to do little things for her.

True lovers constantly find ways to show they appreciate each other and to affirm the relationship they have.

True lovers enjoy each other. They do things together, whether it's working, participating in sports or attending plays and concerts. They share common interests.

True lovers respect each other. They may disagree, but they allow for differences of opinion. When we really love another person, we don't pressure him or her to act contrary to his or her values.

We had a woman in our church who was very talented musically. She once said that people had appreciated her talent for years, but very few had appreciated her as a person. She needed affirmation as a human being and not just recognition of her abilities.

Lovers care by being sensitive to each other's hopes, fears, aspirations, dreams and plans. The apostle John writes, "Beloved, let us love one another" (1 John 4:7, NKJV). "Beloved" could be read as "dear friends," as it is in some translations. He's saying, "As friends, let's love one another."

Lovers respect, love and cherish each other, not only for today but throughout their lives.

Lord God, teach us the full dimensions of love as we discover more about each other and discover more about You. Amen.

To *Love* and to *Cherish*

Sweet Discovery

Kathleen Swartz McQuaig

Taste and see that the LORD is good. (Psalm 34:8)

On the morning of my birthday I caught my newlywed husband hunched over our kitchen counter, carefully studying the directions on a box of cake mix.

Scott and I had been married less than a year. His military duties had taken us far from our Yankee roots, and when it came to celebrating our birthdays, even the warm Georgia sunshine couldn't take the place of our families back in Pennsylvania. Scott did his best to fill the void with kindness.

What my sweet husband lacked in baking experience, he made up in tenacity. He was determined to make it a memorable day. Two decades later I still cherish the memory of his impish smile as he mixed up my birthday surprise.

Scott neared his final preparations with an air of satisfaction. His dimples deepened and he flashed me a broad smile. His warm brown eyes sparkled with the joy and spontaneity of a little child, as if to say, "Look what I did."

I laughed out loud, tickled by his thoughtfulness, thoroughly enjoying his sense of accomplishment. His face shone as he carried two pans of cake batter to the oven.

It was then that I realized that Scott mixed his cake with love, goodness—and a few other things. Sharp points protruded from the batter in the center of each pan. Seeing my quizzical expression, Scott assured me of his attention to detail. "The directions on the box said, 'The cake is done when a toothpick stuck in the center comes out clean.' "

I wrapped my arms around this precious man who was still staring at me with puzzled eyes. Gently I explained that toothpicks are inserted at the *end* of the baking to test the cake's doneness. As the smile I'd been trying to stifle met Scott's, we burst into uncontrollable laughter. It was one sweet discovery!

Thank You, Lord, for the joy and spontaneity that can come when we put tender love above limitations. Amen.

When God Hears

Faye Landrum

For if you forgive men when they sin against you, your heavenly Father will also forgive you. (Matthew 6:14)

For a few weeks that summer my husband was particularly "hard to live with." Bob was excessively critical of me; nothing I did pleased him. He was extremely irritable with the children, producing a mounting tide of resentment in both them and me.

This was just before vacation. I knew Bob was tired from unsolved problems nagging him at work, but knowing this didn't ease the domestic tension that hung over our house like a threatening storm cloud.

One night I went to bed feeling like I couldn't stand it any longer. I retreated into a cocoon of self-pity and sobbed silently. Bob's heavy breathing next to me told me he was asleep and my little episode would go undetected.

I thought about the ways Bob had hurt me lately and how he had been moody and irritable. I even entertained the thought that I might have been better off if I had stayed single.

In the darkness I began to pray that God would help me to tolerate my misery. For quite some time I prayed for the courage, the strength and the grace I thought I needed. I prayed also that God would bring about some sort of change in Bob.

Then, suddenly, I was overcome with a feeling of guilt. My sin of self-pity seemed almost unbearable. My tears flowed even more freely, and I prayed that God would forgive me for my selfish martyrdom, my lack of understanding and my inability to help my husband when he undoubtedly needed me the most. I went to sleep with that prayer in my heart.

A few hours later I was awakened by one of the children needing attention. I was groggy, but as I walked to the bathroom, I was aware that the heavy burden I had been carrying had lifted. I knew God had forgiven me. I knew a change had been wrought within me that would give me the grace of understanding.

The next morning I was still conscious of the exhilaration I had felt during the night. But more wonderful than that was the change in Bob. He talked freely and pleasantly with all of us. The dark cloud of tension had lifted. Even the children noticed the difference.

This was my first experience with the eternal truth that God cannot be reached through a veil of sin. It is only when we bring ourselves to Him and are cleansed by seeking His forgiveness for our own transgressions that we are able to pray for either ourselves or others.

Dear Lord, forgive me when I am selfish or unkind, and help me to forgive the little hurts that come between my husband and me. Amen.

Accentuate the Positive

Jean M. Olsen

And now, dear brothers and sisters . . . fix your thoughts on what is true and honorable and right. Think about things that are pure and lovely and admirable. Think about things that are excellent and worthy of praise . . . and the God of peace will be with you. (Philippians 4:8-9, NLT)

At a recent wedding reception, my husband and I were contestants at a game of *Oldlyweds* (rather than *Newlyweds*). We won the booby prize! The only question we agreed on was "How many sizes larger is your husband's waist now than when you got married?" I knew that answer only because I keep track of his numbers so I can be sure mine are lower than his!

We both had a tough time thinking of *any* answers to questions like "What is his most annoying habit?" or "What was the worst meal she ever cooked?" It was impossible to match our partner's guesswork.

After a lifetime together, why were those questions so difficult? Why couldn't we match responses?

I believe one reason is because we have made a permanent commitment to each other. We never planned an escape route from our marriage. We believed God brought us together for life, and we determined to make it work. Since we accepted one another as we were, we didn't try to make each other over. Well—hardly ever.

I'm thankful for my husband. I'd convinced myself that I'd be an unmarried wallflower all my life. To my amazement, God gave me a Christian husband with life goals almost identical to mine. He even thinks I'm beautiful! (Yes, he wears glasses.) I'm still thrilled and thankful. Irrevocably thankful.

My husband and I don't make a big deal of each other's many blunders and idiosyncrasies. Why should I complain because he leaves the bed messed up after his nap? Why should he get upset because I'm always rearranging the furniture? In the light of five decades of faithfully caring for each other, those negatives aren't worth a whisper.

Lord, enable me always to concentrate on things of good report. Help me to be easy to live with. Amen.

God Knows

Elsie Lippy

Your Father knows what you need. (Matthew 6:8)

Early in our marriage I memorized 168 verses in three months just using the times when I had to wait for my husband. I waited in the car while Bruce made a "quick" stop and after church as he talked with anyone who would respond to his smile and warm "How are you?" I waited while he checked every possible detail of closing up the house before a trip. I waited for him to come home for supper, often imagining he was lying in a ditch somewhere.

On the way to church my husband and I sometimes play the game "God Knows" with three young Mexican-American boys who ride with us.

"God knows how many white lines are on the road to church."

"God knows how many leaves are on that tree."

"God knows when Jesus will come for us."

I was not prepared for the insightful truth that came from our dark-eyed ten-year-old one Sunday morning: "God knows how long Bruce will talk after church today!"

Through the years I've slowly learned, after much prayer, that waiting for my husband is an unchangeable fact of life. Now, most of the time, instead of frantically calling to the Lord, "Please help him to hurry," I plead, "Lord, help me to be patient. Be with Bruce in his endeavors. Make him a blessing to the people he's talking to."

It helps too if I focus on the benefits. I earned an Awana Timothy award for memorizing verses. I never have to worry that we've forgotten anything as we leave for a trip. And I'm making a lot of new friends by proxy!

Along with Bruce's easygoing style of activity—sometimes classified as inactivity—there is often a long waiting period between my question and his answer, or a proposal and his decision.

A friend once told me that I have a mind like a steel trap. When a suggestion is made I'm right on it. Imagine the frustration I feel when I ask my hubby a question and don't even receive a grunt of acknowledgment. I do my best to hold my tongue for ninety seconds, then ask, "W-e-l-l-l-l?" I expectantly listen, only to hear, "I'm thinking."

After twenty-five years of marriage I've realized what God knew all along. He has used this wonderful, loving, detailed man to develop in me the quality of patience—the one I need most of all!

God, I'm so thankful that You haven't let up all these years. You know how I've hurt my testimony at times by not being patient with others. Thank You for giving me just the right husband through whom You could teach me this godly quality. Amen.

My Precious Birthday Banner

Jill Nelson

How precious to me are your thoughts, O God! How vast is the sum of them! (Psalm 139:17)

Plastered across the length of my kitchen wall, this year it announced in rainbow colors, "44 and Ready for More!"

"What do you think, Mom?" my youngest asked proudly. The others trained eager faces on me. Their father was laughing. Our eyes met over their heads. This was *our* moment. The burdens and responsibilities of marriage and family and jobs were light once again.

My birthday banner is tradition—my husband's idea—begun as soon as the first child was old enough to help color the huge letters formed on eight feet of butcher paper. Every year the rhyme is different, but the banner's appearance on the anniversary of my birth is as reliable as the passage of time. I delight to receive these loving messages, crafted with loads of thought, creativity and hilarity. It is always my favorite present. There are years, to my husband's dismay, when it must be my only present.

How do I convey to him my thrill when, a little before my special day, I catch him in a huddle with the kids? I manage to stroll by, and he looks up at me with that wide-eyed, too-innocent stare until I pass out of earshot.

At that moment, it doesn't matter if we still have an unresolved disagreement or financial pressures. My husband has captured a truth from Scripture and applied it to our marriage. His thoughts toward me are many and precious indeed. No wealth is greater or cherishing stronger than to discover oneself the focus of another's loving thoughts.

> *Heavenly Father, our hearts can scarcely comprehend the wonder of Your loving thoughts toward each one of us. Help us to so cherish our spouses that, despite any circumstances in our lives, they never have need to doubt our devotion. Amen.*

To *Love* and to *Cherish*

The Pleasures God Intended

Sue Cameron

May your fountain be blessed, and may you rejoice in the wife of your youth. A loving doe, a graceful deer—may her breasts satisfy you always, may you ever be captivated by her love. (Proverbs 5:18-19)

As a young married woman, I sat at the kitchen table and poured my heart out to my friend about my sexual relationship with my husband. "Linda," I said, "I've got the best husband in the world. He loves me and tells me I'm beautiful. He's tender and kind and is a good provider and father. But I feel like I'm failing him as a lover."

She patted my hand and listened.

I glared at her. "Now you—you enjoy sex. So it's easy for you!"

She nodded and let me continue.

"It's just that he deserves a red-hot lover. He's so perfect and I'm so—so blah!"

My trouble with sex began when I was just a young girl, in about the fifth grade, and a neighbor sexually abused me. My body learned to shut down during arousal, and overcoming that pattern took quite a bit of time, lots of prayer, a clear understanding of God's design and, most of all, patience.

Over time, I learned that God is in favor of really good lovemaking in marriage. He set things up that way. He gave us bodies that respond to a great back rub but not a nose rub. Why? Why did our Creator create certain places with more tactile feeling than others? Love. He loves us—loves you and me and wants us to experience pleasure. Once I understood this it set me on a course to have what God intended me to have.

The Lord also wanted my husband to have a terrific lover—that's me. In the beginning He didn't create Eve and a mistress. No, I'm the only woman in the world that can legitimately fulfill my husband's sexual needs.

And the same is true for him. In fact, God even says in His Word (in First Corinthians 7:4) that my body belongs to my husband and his belongs to me. Wow!

Now, after twenty-four years of marriage, I'm here to tell you that God can work wonders in this area. I'm so glad I didn't give up, didn't settle for life as it was. For many years now I've experienced the pleasure and joy of lovemaking in marriage. And why not? After all, if you're going to do a thing over and over and over and over for the rest of your life, why not enjoy it? Why not become an expert?

So if you were also a victim of sexual abuse—and so many women were—please don't settle for less than God's best in this area. Don't allow your abuser to continue to hold power over your life by stealing from you and your husband the pleasure and closeness that God intended for you to share in your marriage bed. Believe me, it's worth the effort.

Thank You, Father, that You created the sexual relationship for husbands and wives. Thank You too that You can bring healing and wholeness in this area. For those who are hurting who are reading this prayer, I'm asking You to please provide them with the help they need so they can experience the joys You intended. In Jesus' name, Amen.

"I Hope He Chokes on It!"

Pam Halter

And let the wife see that she respects and reverences her husband [that she notices him, regards him, honors him, prefers him, venerates, and esteems him; and that she defers to him, praises him, and loves and admires him exceedingly]. (Ephesians 5:33, AMP)

First, let me make this clear: My husband remarked early in our marriage that he preferred to make his own lunch. "Then I can pack whatever I feel like eating that day," he said. I had no problem with it, because I had enough to take care of in the mornings getting our autistic daughter ready for school. But I did offer.

Several years later, we sat in choir practice waiting for our director to come. I was giving a friend a hard time about parking his car in the pastor's driveway. "That's what's wrong with the world today," I grumbled. "There's no consideration of others. No common courtesy."

Almost immediately I heard my husband's baritone voice. "So where's my lunch every day?"

Everyone laughed. I wanted to sink into the pew, never to be seen again. To this day, I still can't believe he said it! We discussed it on the way home, as you can well imagine. And I packed his lunch that night.

I packed his lunch every night after that until the end of the school year—and every night I muttered, "I hope he chokes on it!"

I also prayed as I packed. Hurt as I was, deep inside I knew my attitude needed changing.

Summer came and summer went. Soon it was time to think about packing lunch again. However, as I got things out and ready, I found I didn't mutter. I even found pleasure in putting things in his lunch that would surprise and please him. Something had happened in my heart that summer.

Gradually I realized that the five minutes it took to pack his lunch turned into five minutes of serving my husband. It takes almost no effort on my part, and almost every day he remarks how good lunch was. Do I always find joy in this small service? No. Some nights, when I'm feeling especially irritated with him, I will "forget" to pack it. I always feel bad about it the next day and promise myself to do better.

To love and to cherish. It's packing a lunch whether I feel like it or not. It's small opportunities of service, small ways to show him I love him—because I really do!

Gentle and patient Lord, continue to develop in me a cherishing of my husband. Remind me that You love and cherish me enough to die for me. Teach me to look at my marriage through Your eyes. Amen.

Love, Honor and Cherish

Steve Dunham

Ye husbands, dwell with them according to knowledge, giving honour unto the wife. (1 Peter 3:7, KJV)

After twenty years of marriage, I thought I knew what marriage is all about. If you had asked me, I would have said that I had been faithful to my wedding vows.

What I would have meant is that I hadn't committed adultery (in a narrow sense, ignoring the lust of the heart that Jesus spoke about). But I wouldn't have been thinking about the words I had spoken on my wedding day so many years before.

It was a book by Bob Moeller called *For Better, for Worse, for Keeps* that made me reflect on the promises I had made to my wife twenty years earlier.

I had promised not only to avoid infidelity but to be faithful. I had promised my wife that I would love, honor and cherish her all the days of my life. These words are stated as a promise, indicating that they are something we have a choice about. I had promised to love, honor and cherish her every day. Reflecting on our life together, I had to admit that I had failed miserably.

Many times I had, in my words and actions, failed to honor my wife, either at home or in public—and it's hard to say which is worse. I had often failed to cherish her and let her know how important she is to me and how much joy and happiness she has brought into my life. Having said that, it's obvious that I had also failed to love her, to put her interests, needs and feelings ahead of my own.

But these are things about which I have a choice. In the past few years I have reflected more often on my wedding vows and made an effort to live up to the promises I made to love, honor and cherish her all the days of my life.

God, give me the grace to be faithful to the promises I made before You, my spouse, our families and our friends on our wedding day. Amen.

Private Spaces

Cec Murphey

And in the morning, a great while before day, he rose and went out to a lonely place, and there he prayed. (Mark 1:35, RSV)

I learned a lot about private spaces from Shirley. One time, only weeks before our marriage, I wanted her to go somewhere with me. "I just need to be alone," she said.

In the months that followed (and in the years since), the importance of private spaces has become clear to me. We need times to separate ourselves, even from the people we love the most. We need moments when we can reflect and integrate what's happening to us.

True love, I learned, makes allowances for private spaces. I've also learned to make private spaces for myself. I do it mostly with running. I go off alone for forty minutes to an hour, usually by myself, and don't want to talk to anyone.

We all need private spaces; some need those spaces more than others. Shirley needs it more than I do, because by nature she's more private. She makes many important decisions in solitude. I like to talk with friends I trust, hear what they say, and then if I'm still not sure, in privacy I decide.

We're all different. True lovers not only understand the differences in each other, but encourage them as well.

In the New Testament, Jesus gave a prime example of private spaces. It says in Mark's Gospel that long before day, He went to a private place and prayed. Afterward the disciples brought sick people to Him and He healed them. He preached everywhere. But first He sought a private space.

Lovers need that private space away from each other and all the crowding noises of the day. We need the opportunity to reflect and to make decisions. In those times of solitude we grow.

Lord of life, help us to encourage each other's private spaces as we mutually seek to follow You. Amen.

On Love

Earlene D. Benson

I have loved you with an everlasting love. (Jeremiah 31:3, NKJV)

When my husband and I were married in 1948, we knew little about each other. He soon discovered that although I was familiar with the terms *broom* and *mop* and had a vague idea of the functions of these items, I didn't realize they were to be used on a consistent basis. He also didn't know that in the twenty-five years and six months before we were married, I had cooked only *one* meal. That was for a former boyfriend.

The corn had been OK. It came from a can. The mashed potatoes, always white, fluffy mounds when my mother had made them, were somewhat soggy and faintly green. The box-mix chocolate pudding was, as my boyfriend told me, the consistency of the heavy tar used to patch roads in those days. My father had taught me to broil steak properly, so the meal wasn't a complete disaster. As it was, though, I never cooked again until I was married.

Norm should have suspected that, since I was an only child who was orphaned at seventeen and who had been independent for eight years, words like *cooperation* would be foreign to my nature. Of course, I had two uncles as guardians until I was twenty-one, but they were in Ohio. I was in New York, so most day-to-day decisions were mine to make without consulting anyone or asking permission.

The controlling force that has made this marriage successful is Norm's commitment to Ephesians 5:25: "Husbands, love your wives, just as Christ loved the church." He accepted my weaknesses patiently, has never stopped loving me and has eaten whatever I prepare without complaint. Today I am considered a good cook and my independent nature is tamed. Now, if only I were sure what to do with a broom!

Dear Lord, thank You for Norm and his commitment to making our marriage work and for his desire to dwell on my strengths rather than my weaknesses. Amen.

Seek and Pursue

Brandy S. Brow

Depart from evil and do good; seek peace and pursue it. (Psalm 34:14, NKJV)

Jim sat on the couch beside me staring at a Discovery Health Channel rerun while I folded another infant sleeper and mindlessly gazed at the TV . . . waiting. *When will he turn that thing off? He always says I don't make time for him, but when I'm here he never does anything.*

Night after night my husband and I followed this pattern, thinking that peace and harmony would appear in the absence of verbal contention. Yet both of us felt empty from our lack of communication, and our unspoken contention grew. We prayed every night for peace to fill our home, but it didn't.

One night, after being frustrated over another evening of silent companionship, God brought to remembrance the second half of Psalm 34:14, "Seek peace and pursue it." The evening's events replayed in my mind. We individually sought peace by making ourselves readily available to the other. The problem was, I waited for Jim to act while he waited for me, and neither of us knew it. If we didn't begin to pursue one another, our marriage was going to fall apart before our eyes.

God didn't want me to wait any longer for my husband to act first, even if I thought Jim should. He wanted me to put down my agenda first to pursue doing something with Jim, be it read the Bible, help complete a chore or play a game.

At first I argued with God. It was difficult to stop being selfish all the time, and I didn't like it. But when I resigned to obeying God, things happened. He changed my thinking from "What can Jim do with me?" to "What can I do with Jim?" My husband responded when I pursued him, and the empty feeling left. After many nights of frustrated, silent companionship, peace finally could embrace us.

Don't wait. Begin pursuing marital peace today.

Holy God, please help us put down our agendas to pursue communication and activities with our spouses, even if we think they should put down their things to be with us first. As we do, may Your peace enter our marriages and prevail. Thank You, Jesus. Amen.

Rare and Beautiful Treasures
BaBette Z. Bechtold

By wisdom a house is built, and through understanding it is established; through knowledge its rooms are filled with rare and beautiful treasures. (Proverbs 24:3-4)

My husband is one of the most even-tempered people I know. While we were dating I was drawn to his patience and his calm under fire. Funny how the thing you most admire about your spouse can quickly turn into an irritant. It wasn't long after we were married that I dubbed him the "Ice Man." In time I came to see his calm as just plain cold, his patience as passive indifference. I was hurt by his repeated stoic responses to things he had done that deeply hurt me, and I felt he didn't care about my feelings. Things were definitely frosty between us.

Over the course of several months I struggled to remain open and free of anger and bitterness. Some days I won; other days I didn't. The days I didn't were filled with tormenting thoughts, anguish and a sharp tongue. Our home was filled with tension. It was a daily battle to trust and believe that my husband loved me, but instinctively I knew if I succumbed to the temptation to lay the first brick down around my heart in order to "protect" it, in time that wall would divide our home. I certainly didn't want my children suffering the agony of divorce like I had, and so I wrestled on.

Learning to understand and respect each other's unique way of seeing things didn't happen overnight. Over time I was led to godly resources that gave me the knowledge I needed to understand him—and to understand myself. I found out that I need verbal affirmation to feel loved, and that he shows love by doing acts of service. Just that simple revelation allowed me to see and hear my husband's love in the ways he was showing me—and the ways he intended. I grew to trust him and appreciate that every time he wiped off the kitchen counter or filled my car with gas he was saying, "I love you, honey."

With God's help we can change the way we see our spouses and have the courage to lay aside the stones of hurt and anger. We can choose to build our homes in wisdom, not anger, and fill them with the rare and beautiful treasures of acceptance and security that are born out of understanding.

> *Lord, give us the courage to lay aside our hurt and anger and choose to forgive. Give us new ways of seeing each other so that we might have strong homes built on love. Lead us to the resources that give us the knowledge we need to choose to fill our homes with the rare and beautiful treasures of acceptance and understanding, that our homes might be firmly established beacons to the world of Your love. Amen.*

To *Love* and to *Cherish*

A Glimpse of God

Dianne E. Butts

*Let your light shine before men, that they may see your good deeds and
praise your Father in heaven.* (Matthew 5:16)

I stood in the street gazing at the thick black mark down the side
of my car. It had been a stupid thing to do, and it was all my fault.
I had a zillion errands to run on my lunch hour. In my haste, I
wheeled into an empty parking spot, cutting the wheel too soon
and too sharp and sideswiping the next car over.

Thankfully, there was no damage to the other car—just a
shiny spot on the bumper's black rubber where I'd rubbed the
mud off. But that black rubber left a thick mark down the side of
my car. What would Hal, my husband, say? *Will he be angry?* I
wondered. *Will he be disgusted at my carelessness? Will he be frustrated
with the damage I've done in my haste?*

That evening I took him outside and showed him the car.

"These things happen," he said with a shrug. He headed back
toward the house.

"Wait a minute," I protested. "Look at what I did."

He shrugged again.

"Aren't you mad?" I asked.

"No," he said. Seeing my concern, he finally bent down for a
closer inspection of the damage. "I think most of it will rub out,"
he offered.

I stood there amazed at my husband's reaction—or lack of one, actually. Past experiences with other people had caused me to fear my husband's reaction. But he didn't react like other people. Instead, he loved me—despite what I had done.

Someone has said that God teaches us about His love through our spouses. I can testify to that truth. Hal's patient love through the years has taught me to trust in God. He will stick with me no matter what. Because I've learned I don't have to be afraid when I mess up, I am encouraged to discover and to be who I truly am—with all my faults and foibles.

Hal has given me a most precious gift. Terms such as "unconditional love" seemed vague, intangible and elusive . . . until Hal gave me a real glimpse of what it means to experience God's unconditional love.

Lord, help me to live before my husband and all others in such a way that they will see glimpses of You in my attitudes and actions. Let Your kindness, gentleness, patience and unconditional love shine through me in a way that will draw others to You. Amen.

Called to Be Intimate

Wanda G. Schwandt

The husband must fulfill his duty to his wife, and likewise also the wife to her husband. (1 Corinthians 7:3, NASB)

I dropped into bed like a lead weight in water. In between changing diapers, making meals, running errands, doing laundry and cleaning floors, my young ones hung on me and ran me ragged. They were in bed now, and the fatiguing day had finally come to an end. Now it was a supreme effort just to pull the covers up over my shoulders.

As he climbed into bed next to me, my husband slipped his arms around me and kissed my ear. I bristled at his touch and pushed him away. "Please don't," I whimpered.

"What's wrong? We haven't snuggled in a while." Hurt and irritation were evident in his voice.

"I'm exhausted, that's all. I just can't."

"You are always too tired," he said as he rolled over.

Facing his back, I silently sobbed. We had had this conversation hundreds of times before. I wanted to show him my love, but I had nothing left to give.

In Ephesians 5:28-31 and First Corinthians 7:3-5, God called husbands and wives to be intimate in both body and soul, devoted to meeting the needs of the other. In Song of Solomon 5:1, God blessed the marriage union and encouraged the lovers to enjoy the blessing of intimacy. It was not meant to be a burden. So what was blocking us from sharing in that joy?

I began to realize that avoiding intimacy was only the tip of the iceberg. Many unfulfilled needs separated us. Schedules and workloads were out of balance. We needed to communicate and compromise in order for both of us to have our needs met.

Nudging my husband awake, I suggested we make time to talk the next day, which we did. During our discussion, we talked about my need for some quiet time before I could devote myself to his needs. I needed him to care for the kids for at least an hour every evening, allowing me some restful peace and quiet. In turn, he expressed his need to feel welcome and appreciated at the end of a mind-numbing day. He asked me to liberally dole out hugs and kisses and smiles in the evening. Plus, we agreed to set aside regular times to talk. After putting those small changes into practice, fulfilling each other's needs became a joy, both in the bedroom and out.

Author of Love, thank You for creating multiple ways to express love for one another. Continue to teach us how to love and be loved, creating a union that exudes joy and gives glory to Your name. Amen.

Boy, Can He Get on My Nerves!

Vicki Smith

Beloved, let us love one another, for love is of God; and everyone who loves is born of God and knows God. (1 John 4:7, NKJV)

Even after thirty-two years of marriage he can still get on my nerves—and that's quite a feat! After all, I have a wonderful husband. He likes to shop and to cook. He shares his deepest feelings with me. He makes our bed (back surgeries make my mornings difficult).

But boy, can he get on my nerves!

Like the time we drove home from a one-week family visit. Four of the eight hours we rode in silence. (For me to sit for any length of time without speaking is unusual.) For two of those long four hours, I sat in the same seat of the same car, tears streaming down my cheeks, and he never even noticed. This silent trip uncorked an already full reservoir of hormonal emotions.

Boy, can he get on my nerves!

The "fight" had been building for days—even weeks. This vacation was needed. We were tired before we left home, and we were even more tired as we returned. The visit with three precious grandchildren had only served to escalate the tension between us.

Once home, we unloaded the car and sat face-to-face. We began to talk. And talk. And talk. In this wonderful time (looking back I can say wonderful), God revealed an old and fundamental lesson.

As newlyweds we went on a Marital Maintenance Weekend annually. After our children were born, Grandma always came to babysit for us. However, when the kids grew and left home, we thought we no longer needed to get away. After all, we were alone in the house all the time now.

Today our schedules are busier than ever. The career workload is at its peak. We are doing things we had dreamed about as a young married couple. When we do get away, we travel to play with grandkids or to visit aging parents. Our Marital Maintenance Weekend has been lost.

The need to focus on each other and to share our feelings is still central to our marriage. We need to spend more quality time together. And so, we will be booking our annual Marital Maintenance Weekend without grandkids, without aging parents and without imposing schedules next year, and the next and the next and the next. . . .

Dear Father, hold us in Your arms as we hold each other in ours. May our love for one another continue to grow as our love for You flourishes. In the name of the greatest love, Jesus, Amen.

Praying for Our Lovers

Cec Murphey

And so we keep on praying for you, that our God will make you worthy of the life to which he called you. And we pray that God, by his power, will fulfill all your good intentions and faithful deeds. (2 Thessalonians 1:11, NLT)

Each day I pray for Shirley. I don't pray for her only out of habit. I talk to God about her because of my love for her. I want Shirley to be the very best Christian that she can be. I recognize talents in her which God has given, and I want them to be perfected. I recognize weaknesses in her that I want to see corrected.

I think that is the intent of Paul's words when he wrote that he prayed for the Thessalonians. He prayed for them to be worthy of the Christian life, to be filled with God's power, to be perfect in the work of faith.

Lovers also pray like that. When we love someone, we want that person to be as perfect as possible. We care about every area of the other's life. I think Shirley is a better person today than she was when we first met. She's more in touch with herself, more in harmony with Jesus Christ. Part of her growth has come about because I have supported her in all kinds of ways, but especially through prayer.

Lovers pray for each other because they are important to each other.

Shirley and I both realized early in our relationship that we made a wholesome trio—God, Shirley and me. We learned that we could talk to each other, and then we could talk to God about each other. Often we pray for God to increase our love and our understanding. We pray for patience. We learn to take our problems to God together. Prayer has been a very exciting and special part of our life together.

Holy God, thank You that You hear our prayers as we pray for each other and as we grow in unity. Amen.

Speaking of Tongues

June Eaton

Set a guard, O LORD, over my mouth; keep watch over the door of my lips. (Psalm 141:3, NKJV)

Many times I had read that Scripture. Never did I dream that it could apply to me, but I had the rhythm of the city in my bones and frequently acted on impulse. My husband, on the other hand, was from a rural area, where life went on at a slower pace. He was quiet and deliberate—in fact, that was part of what attracted me to him. Conversation was not one of his strong points. Someone would ask him a question, and what seemed to me an unbearable silence followed.

Say something—anything! I found myself thinking.

Afraid my friends and family would think my groom was either hard of hearing or rude, I began jumping into the conversation and answering for him. Or I would repeat the question and prompt him for answers. He was too polite to protest.

I continued this habit for many months before my dad caught me in the act one day. "Can't Fred speak for himself?" he asked gently.

I was horrified to realize what I had been doing. By my actions, I was usurping my husband's role as head of our home and implying that he wasn't capable of thinking and acting for himself.

"Lord, help me to guard my lips," I prayed desperately. *From now on,* I vowed, *when someone asks my husband a question, I will bite down hard on my tongue, clamp my lips shut and count to ten.*

It didn't always work. When I got to the count of ten and he still hadn't replied, the impulse was still there to intercede for him. After a while, I succeeded in keeping quiet—some of the time—until Fred could fire off an answer. But then I began to think, *He's not telling it right*, and I'd come up with my own more dramatic rendition.

I repeated Psalm 141:3 over and over in my mind until my jaw felt like it was permanently locked. But gradually my offending habit began to subside, and guarding my tongue through what seemed insufferable pauses and silences finally paid off. Fred found his voice.

Over time, we learned to accommodate each other. He speeded up his reactions and I slowed mine down. Now, after thirty-nine years of marriage, the tables have turned. When we are out in public, it is my husband who does most of the talking. I use my lips to smile at the head of our home instead of answering for him.

Thank You, Lord, for teaching me to guard my tongue and to appreciate the things Fred says when I give him the opportunity. Amen.

I Love Getting Flowers!

Kathy Collard Miller

The wise woman builds her house, but with her own hands the foolish one tears hers down. (Proverbs 14:1)

"Our fourth wedding anniversary is in a few days," I mused as I sat down, more and more aware of my bulging stomach. I was pregnant with our first child, and I didn't feel very good about myself. It was hard to consider myself sexy or desirable. Sometimes I wondered if Larry still looked at me the same way. *If he would buy me flowers this anniversary, that would really let me know he does,* I thought to myself.

As June 20 got closer and closer, my hopes for flowers increased even though he had seldom bought me flowers. *He should know how important this is to me,* I reasoned. *I'm sure he'll come through.*

June 20 finally arrived. Unexpectedly, the doorbell rang. I opened the door to find a florist delivery boy holding a beautiful spray of long-stemmed red roses. It was gorgeous! My heart beat with excitement. *He does love me,* I thought. *He actually thought of it himself!*

I was eager to open the card and see the romantic words Larry had written.

"Congratulations on choosing us to build your new pool," the card read. "We know you'll love it."

The flowers weren't from Larry at all—they were from the pool company with whom we had contracted to build our pool the previous week!

Suddenly I started laughing. "Lord, You do have a sense of humor. You allowed these flowers to arrive on my anniversary so I wouldn't be too disappointed when Larry arrives home empty-handed. I see now how unrealistic my thinking is."

I had known Larry hated giving me flowers because he didn't like the fact that they died. I just couldn't convince him they were valuable to me—by just receiving them—even if they did die.

As the years passed, Larry's attitude stayed the same. But several years ago, after twenty-three years of marriage, Larry planned something that totally surprised me. We were speaking at a Valentine's Day banquet for couples. Near the end of our presentation, Larry began talking about our different opinions about flowers—which wasn't part of our planned talk. I stood there, wondering what in the world he was doing.

Then Larry pulled out from within the podium, where he had hidden it earlier, an exquisite real rose covered in 24k gold. As the audience clapped in delight, I was caught totally off guard. I leaned over and gave him a tender kiss.

That rose sits in a glass vase on my desk as a constant reminder that even old husbands can learn new tricks.

Father God, thank You that there is always hope for my marriage. You promise to meet all our true needs, and I trust You to meet all my true needs in my marriage. Amen.

[From *When the Honeymoon's Over: Building a Real-Life Marriage*, © 1997 Kathy Collard Miller. Published by Waterbrook Press.]

Intimate Conversation

Paula Harris

Death and life are in the power of the tongue. (Proverbs 18:21, NKJV)

Like an overinflated balloon, our conversation grew more and more intense until finally . . . POW! That moment the conversation abruptly ended. My bulwark husband flopped into a chair like a collapsed pile of rubble. His saddened eyes resembled a disciplined puppy. His sigh spewed forth exasperation. Then silence permeated the room. He was doubled over. I was, standing still, though my heart was racing. Neither he nor I said a word. I realized I had gone too far.

A whisper from God broke the silence. "Paula, why do you justify acting this way with him in the name of intimacy?" Our Lord knew this behavior was a result of my viewpoint on intimacy within a marriage. I believed a couple was truly intimate if they could divulge anything to their spouses and receive empathy in return. Little did I know that this question would teach me a profound lesson I would never forget.

Suddenly I saw that my behavior reflected that of a black widow spider who kills her mate. It was not intentional, nor deliberate, on my part. Yet I was slowing killing my hubby just the same. It finally struck me as I focused on his countenance that I was the only one benefitting from these conversations. I could walk away with my burden lifted and feel refreshed. He, on the other hand, was left empty. This style of conversing was draining him. Although intimacy makes it possible for a couple to share in a way they would not share with another, inappropriate expressions about disappointment, anger, fear or misunderstanding can harm a relationship.

With a renewed sensitivity, I knelt down at eye level with him and asked his forgiveness for the way I had spoken. For a moment, there was complete silence again. Then he warmly wrapped me in his arms. That was the beginning of a higher level of intimacy I had almost forfeited.

Lord, thank You for my husband, who has been so loving and patient with me. I am also thankful for Your forgiveness of the way I've conducted myself at times in the secrecy of my home. I would never talk that way to others. From this day forward, let my words speak life and not death to him. I realize the precious intimacy between the two of us is a reflection of the intimacy I share with You. I praise You for the continuous change You have wrought in my life. Amen.

Love Will Remain

Sue Cameron

And now these three remain: faith, hope and love. But the greatest of these is love. (1 Corinthians 13:13)

After fifteen years of marriage I discovered that my husband, Craig, has this . . . habit. He reminds me of love! Like on Tuesday night at 6:30 p.m. when Bible study meets in our home at 7.

I am frantic. Frantically throwing dishes into the dishwasher, fanatically issuing orders: "Josh, Sara, Aimee, Eric, finish your homework and go upstairs!"

"But Mom," says Eric, "I'm only in kindergarten. I don't have homework."

"Then help Josh with his!" I scream.

"But Mom," says Josh, "I'm in seventh grade. I don't think he can help me much."

I scowl at both of them.

That's when Craig strolls into the kitchen. Cool, calm, collected. I thrust the coffee pot into his hands. "Make the coffee," I demand. But he doesn't. He puts the pot down, takes me into his arms and tells me I'm beautiful. He likes the looks of a harried woman.

Normally I would sigh and impatiently roll my eyes at him. But not tonight. Tonight, after fifteen years of being loved when I'm a raging maniac, a wonderful truth begins to sink in. Although he's never said it in words, Craig is reminding me of an eternal truth. Love is the greatest of all. Love will remain. Dirty dishes won't remain. Hectic moments won't remain. The self-imposed pressure of this hour won't remain. Love will. Love is the important thing. Let's not miss this moment. Let's enjoy the love.

So, in an uncommon response, instead of yelling at my husband to "help me do all this stuff," I kiss him back. It is nice. I think it is better than yelling.

The coffee gets made. The dishes get washed. And I am reminded that this moment is worth enjoying because love will always remain.

Father God, thank You that You always take time to show us how much You love us. Help me to take time to respond to Your love. And please help me to take time in my marriage to show and tell my husband how much I love him. Thank You for the gift of affection, and help me to show warm and tender affection to my husband. Amen.

PART SEVEN

Till Death Do Us Part

"*I Will Never Leave Thee*"

Marcia A. Gruver

For I am persuaded, that neither death, nor life, nor angels, nor principalities, nor powers, nor things present, nor things to come, nor height, nor depth, nor any other creature, shall be able to separate us from the love of God, which is in Christ Jesus our Lord. (Romans 8:38-39, KJV)

"OK, that's it. I'm out of here." How many times had I said it? Oh, there were variations: "If you do that again, I'm gone," or, "I won't be here when you get home," and, of course, "I can't take this anymore. I'm leaving."

I followed through a few times. I packed my car with the essentials: clothes, shoes, cosmetics, jewelry, photo albums, computer, computer monitor, printer and television set. I burst in on my poor mother with all my possessions, sobbing that my marriage was over, only to pack up the car and slink back home before nightfall.

One time I really showed him. I rented a house behind his back. I had the lights turned on, a phone put in and groceries stocked in the pantry. He went out of town, and I moved out. I sat in that cold, lonely little cracker box, warming myself with thoughts of how shocked and saddened he would be when he found me gone. To my surprise, he seemed to do OK without me. So I moved back home.

This went on for the first three years of our marriage. The smallest thing could go wrong and I would leave or threaten to.

Why? The truth is, I don't know. I loved him very much and I was happy with him. Maybe it was fear caused by past rejection. You know, leave him before he leaves me. Or maybe it was chronic immaturity complicated by persistent stupidity. It doesn't matter. That's not the story here.

This is about how God changed me. God cured me by sending a man into my life who I couldn't chase away with a stick. My husband is solid as a rock in his commitment to me. I soon learned he would not beg me to stay, but he would never ask me to go. And he would never leave me. No matter what.

Lee has "put on" Christ, as mentioned in Galatians 3:27, and he wears Him well. My husband always took me back without reproach, though it hurt him when I left or talked of leaving.

God used my husband to teach me what it means to keep a vow. Lee meant it when he promised, "Till death do us part." Hurt and rejected people have a hard time with the concept of love as described in Romans 8:38-39. God sent me a living, breathing picture of His unfathomable, unshakable love.

Father, thank You for the promise in Hebrews 13:5 that You will never leave us or forsake us. Help us to follow Your example and make that same commitment to our mates. Amen.

Jesus Loves Me in the Winter

Leslie Trent Conger

For everything there is a season . . . a time to weep, and a time to laugh; a time to mourn, and a time to dance. (Ecclesiastes 3:1, 4, RSV)

We were there, as many of us as could be, gathered around my stepfather as he lay fighting for his last breaths—brothers and sisters, stepbrothers and stepsisters, our spouses and my mother—at Papa's right side. He had been a loving and wise father and pastor of God's flock, beloved by all who knew him. Two years after he lost his first wife to cancer, he married my mother, who had been a widow for fourteen years.

How we had rejoiced in this tender relationship that burgeoned like spring and burst into the full bloom of a vibrant summer pageantry of love! After five years together, however, his health fell away like autumn leaves, and now we faced the chill of winter's call. As we walked with him to the gate of death, my mother spoke words of relinquishment. The gate opened, bid him come inside and closed quickly behind him. We were left in stunned grief. As much as I knew that I had lost my second father, what really broke my heart was watching my mother say good-bye.

Not a day goes by that I do not wonder what life would be like without my husband, Alan. Having lost two fathers, one by accident in the prime of his life and the other by illness in older age, I am fully aware of life's possibilities. Sometimes it is hard for me to let Alan go fishing—I worry about his safety. I am concerned that he eats well and exercises so that he will prolong his good health. Mostly, though, I try to remember that every day I have him is a day to enjoy him, to encourage him and to receive the love he has for me. Every evening then brings an opportunity to thank God for His gift to me in Alan.

It does me no good to clutch at those I love, for ultimately death will wrest them away and leave me face-to-face with the only relationship I can ever fully possess—that of myself and God. My Creator and Redeemer has promised to be with me always. Nothing can separate me from His love—not the death of my beloved, not even my own death. Am I fearful of being alone? I needn't be. If I am in a season of fullness, I must enjoy God's gifts and enjoy Him in the midst of it. Then, if winter's chill calls Alan away, I will already know the certainty of God's presence and be able to receive His comfort.

Father, thank You for Your love, which abides with us in every season of our lives. Today we enjoy the season of married love. When winter requires us to relinquish summer, comfort us in the knowledge that in Your time, mourning will become the dance of spring. Amen.

A Special Anniversary

Faye Landrum

So don't be anxious about tomorrow. God will take care of your tomor-row too. Live one day at a time. (Matthew 6:34, TLB)

My husband was terminally ill with bone cancer. As our forty-second wedding anniversary drew near, I found myself both looking forward to it and dreading it at the same time. What could I do to make that day special for the one I had lived with and loved for more than four decades?

Bonnie, one of my best friends, called me a few days before the anticipated date. "I know next week is your anniversary," she said, "and since you can't go out to dinner, Tom and I will bring dinner to you."

As we continued talking, she outlined a plan. "We will supply the food, but we won't stay to eat with you. Anniversary dinners should be eaten alone."

After we finished talking, I told Bob about the arrangement. "Isn't that great?" I said. "We can have a special anniversary din-ner together after all." I tried to sound happy and excited, hop-ing he would be pleased.

Bob turned his head away from me. Tears moistened his eyes. "I can't do anything for you this year," he faltered.

In forty-two years, he had never once forgotten our anniver-sary. Always he had taken me to dinner at a special restaurant and had a card and a small gift for me. I knew it hurt him deeply that this year he could do nothing.

As I took his hand, I cried too. "Honey, we're together," I said. "That's all that matters."

At noon on our "special day," Tom and Bonnie arrived with dinner. They also supplied a vase of fresh flowers, pink-and-blue cloth place mats and special anniversary napkins. We had all the trimmings for a special celebration.

Tom and Bonnie also supplied us with cards for each other— one for each of us to give to the other. I knew they had chosen the cards carefully. The verses were lighthearted with a touch of humor but serious in their messages of love.

I put Bob's dinner on his over-the-bed stand, and I sat on the opposite twin bed with a TV tray for my table. As we enjoyed our dinner, I tried to make light conversation and talk about the night of our wedding forty-two years before.

When we finished our anniversary dinner, I produced our wedding album and my bride's book. Together we reviewed pictures of the rainy night when we were married. I had dressed in a room at the back of the church, then walked outside to the sanctuary. One of the pictures in the album showed Bob's best man and an usher holding a raincoat over my head as I lifted my skirts to scurry up the stairs.

Even though we both knew this would be our last anniversary together, the pain was kept at a minimum. By remembering the joy we had shared in the past, we were able to hurdle the pain of the present. It is the present in which God's grace is sufficient. His name is I AM—not I WAS or I WILL BE.

Thank You, Jesus, that we can trust You to take care of our tomorrows.
And thank You for the friends You supply to help us along the way. Amen.

The Three of Us

Jean Pence

And if one can overpower him who is alone, two can resist him. A cord of three strands is not quickly torn apart. (Ecclesiastes 4:12, NASB)

My husband's whisper awakened me out of a sound sleep: "I have to go to the bathroom." I shook myself awake and reached for the zipper on our tent flap. Quietly we crawled past our five-year-old daughter, sound asleep on her cot, and out into the rain-flooded woods. Virtually blind without his contact lenses, my husband clutched my arm and shuffled along next to me, afraid of falling over something in this unfamiliar world. At the age of thirty-five he rarely needed my help for such a routine activity. Laughter bubbled up in each of us at the picture we made stumbling along together.

In that moment my mind flashed ahead fifty years to a time when helping my husband to the restroom could become a daily necessity. I tightened my hand on his arm, startled by the fierce wave of protectiveness that washed over me. We had suffered through some hard times in our marriage, and the love that we shared seemed so frail. At times I was consumed with worry about whether that love would hold in the future.

As we continued walking, the sense of protectiveness that I felt lingered. It raised a new hope in me. In that moment I felt a deep and unshakable love for my husband that I knew came from my heavenly Father.

God would furnish the strength as well as the love I needed to see me through any situation in our marriage. He expected me to love my husband forever, and I could expect Him to provide me with that love. Alone, the two of us might stumble and fail, but together the three us would make it through whatever was to come.

Heavenly Father, I praise You for creating this beautiful relationship of husband and wife. I praise You for standing beside and between my husband and me and for giving each of us the strength to guide, protect and love the other. Thank You that with Your power it is possible to love forever. Amen.

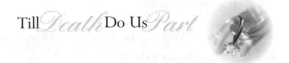

Always Together

Gwen Northcutt

Therefore shall a man leave his father and his mother, and shall cleave unto his wife: and they shall be one flesh. (Genesis 2:24, KJV)

The first sign was fatigue. So unusual for Larry! At age seventy-six, he vigorously cared for our two-acre garden, fruit trees, flowers and the love of his life, his nature trail—a park setting of azaleas, rhododendron, ferns and wild flowers separated by cart paths.

Larry finally agreed to see a doctor. It took three months of tests before the diagnosis was made: congestive heart failure. Incredible! Not Larry, the perennial picture of health! But it was true.

The next two years were spent in and out of doctors' offices and/or the hospital. Larry felt so bad he didn't even complain about my driving. He kept promising me, "I am going to make it!" His cheerful, optimistic attitude was evident in his hearty response, "Great!" when asked how he felt. One day the doctor asked, and Larry answered, "Terrible!" We knew the tide had turned.

We had talked tentatively about moving into a retirement community. As Larry cast loving, longing glances through the sun room windows at his beloved land, I knew he could not leave it. The scene from those windows changed with the seasons as he got weaker.

During his last hospitalization, a hospice social worker visited us. Larry was indignant! When she gave him the choice of going into a nursing home or going home with hospice, he fairly screamed, "A nursing home?" With his bushy, expressive eyebrows shooting up and down, he proclaimed, "I will have you know I have no intention of leaving this planet any time soon." We did go home with hospice, and he did leave this planet two and a half weeks later—most reluctantly.

Larry's illness bonded us even closer. His weakened condition made it difficult for him to talk, and my hearing loss made it difficult for me to hear. Therefore, much of our communication was wordless. After fifty-six years of marriage, who needed words? Looks spoke volumes. We held hands as love, strength and understanding flowed between us.

My long-ago vision of us walking together hand-in-hand into the sunset was being fulfilled. The sunset of our life together was more gorgeous than I could have imagined. Dark spots and streaks appeared against the vibrant colors, of course, but only served to intensify their brilliance.

As I felt him slipping away, the wrenching pain of separation was suddenly replaced by a sense of joy that Larry was in his home, that I was with him and that even this final experience was one we were sharing.

Larry did not leave alone. A part of me went with him—and a part of him remains with me. Parting really is such sweet sorrow. And I will see him on the morrow.

Lord God, thank You for choosing Larry to be my husband and for making us truly one flesh. Even death did not separate us completely. Amen.

A Test of Dedication

Brenda R. Coats

It is a snare to a man to utter a vow [of consecration] rashly and [not until] afterward inquire [whether he can fulfill it]. (Proverbs 20:25, AMP)

"Well, someone had to finish raising you," friends and family often joke, referring to how young I was when we married. My husband, who is five years my senior, doesn't receive the same friendly bantering, other than an occasional "cradle robber" remark—usually from me!

While seventeen is certainly a young age to wed, it seemed irrelevant at the time. We were in love! Those around us seemed skeptical, but we were sincerely dedicated, looking forward to living the rest of our lives together. "Don't worry about what others think," my future husband would advise. "We both know we're in this forever. That's all that matters."

The test of dedication came two years and two children later, when the realities of what it takes to make marriage and family a success hit hard and we no longer had the time to be in love. I was swimming (sometimes drowning) in laundry and dirty diapers. Sleepless nights became the norm, and my youthful freedom turned into overwhelming responsibilities. An emotional distance crept into the marriage, and at one point my husband revealed, "I don't feel like you want to be around me anymore."

My heart ached at the pain I'd caused, adding to my inner struggles.

I found myself faced with a decision. I could stay true to my vows and do my best to experience the joy God intended for marriage, or I could abandon them. Prayer, coupled with an outpouring of unconditional love on my husband's part, enabled me to make the right choice, though at times my heart cried otherwise. "I'm stickin' with you, no matter what," he would often encourage. Though simple words, they effectively revealed his deep dedication to me. Who could resist a heart like that?

A decade later, I am able to look back on that trial with a thankful heart, because it fueled and strengthened my desire to be committed. "Till death do us part." With God as my Helper, those are the words I will embrace and act on, both now and in the future—whatever it may hold.

> *Lord, trials will inevitably make their way into my marriage. When they do, please give me the strength and resolve to remain true to the vows I have made to both You and my spouse. Amen.*

My Turn

Sharon Bridgewater

And let us not lose heart and grow weary and faint in acting nobly and doing right, for in due time and at the appointed season we shall reap, if we do not loosen and relax our courage and faint. (Galatians 6:9, AMP)

The wheelchair moved along the rough path, my husband gently guiding it. Mom sat slumped over, her vacant eyes no longer searching the fall colors she had once loved. My dearest mother was present in body only.

Dad and I followed, talking quietly in case Mom could understand. Talking was not something my father and I did easily. All communications of the past had gone through my mother, for we knew the answers would be bathed in loving wisdom. Now words caused me to pull my coat up around my throat as a chill hit me. Dad spelled out the gradual deterioration of the once vibrant woman. Stories of disintegrating words, uncontrolled bodily functions and the inability to swallow shook me to the core. Her life was fading before our eyes, and I feared for her future.

As far as I knew, my parents' marriage had never been a brilliant one. I assumed it had been held together by my mother's faith. I had always laid a certain amount of blame on this man who walked beside me—blame for not expressing his love, blame for supplying only physical needs, blame for the shortcomings I found within myself. Now my mother was completely in his hands, and I wondered about her fate. Would a dark corner in a rest home hall make up my mother's last days?

"It's hard, Sis," he was saying. "Everything has to be done for her now. She doesn't even have the ability to smile anymore. But you know, I was thinking about it the other day, and I remembered the wedding vows Mom and I took some sixty-two years ago—for better, for worse, in sickness and in health."

I almost stopped in the path, immobilized by the unfamiliar sentiments coming from my dad.

"I made those promises all those years ago, and I intend to keep them. She's taken care of me. It's my turn to take care of her."

A deep breath of relief escaped as we continued our walk under the falling leaves. I realized the seal of my parents' marriage had been commitment. Whether it was guilt or love or some other equally strong emotion, my dad was making a commitment of sacrifice to keep his vows to his once beautiful bride. Commitment had been stronger than everything that had come against them throughout the years of their marriage. Now commitment would see my mom through the time remaining, with my dad at her side.

Father God, help us to remember our vows and to reach down deeply for the determination to keep them. No matter what comes our way, may we always keep our word to each other. Amen.

A Better Day Tomorrow

Georgia E. Burkett

For we know that when . . . we die and leave these bodies—we will have wonderful new bodies in heaven, homes that will be ours forevermore, made for us by God himself. (2 Corinthians 5:1, TLB)

"I'll see you tomorrow, hon. I know I'll feel better then." My husband's whispered farewell as I left his hospital bed that sultry summer evening was surely meant to cheer me. Even so, Dewey's sunken eyes and labored breathing were evidence that his time on earth was almost over.

Although his doctors had told him that his illness was terminal, Dewey jokingly bantered their predictions with, "No, sir, I'm never going to die." He was referring to his spiritual body, of course. But he also wanted those doctors, and everyone else, to know that as long as there was breath in his body, he was going to enjoy every moment God gave him here on earth. And he was determined that I enjoy it with him.

I cried myself to sleep that night as Dewey's labored good night repeated itself over and over in my mind. How could I ever face life without him? He had always been by my side—my friend, my lover and a mighty shrewd businessman. But when I thought of the pain he was suffering with such bravado, I could do no other than pray that God would soon take him home to be with Him.

Many times during the forty-four years of our marriage we had talked about our future home in heaven. We wondered how we would look when we met Jesus face-to-face and how He would look. Now Dewey would soon know the answer.

The Bible tells us in Philippians 3:21 that Jesus will change our dying bodies into glorious bodies like His own. So, even though losing Dewey would be like losing a part of myself, I would have been unpardonably selfish to ask God to keep him imprisoned in agony. God had a brand-new, pain-free body planned for him—one that would endure forever.

Dewey's "better day tomorrow" arrived early the next morning. As I looked upon his lifeless form, I could well imagine his face brightening with delight as he met Jesus. And I could almost hear him say, "Hey, hon, didn't I tell you I was going to feel better tomorrow? I'll be waiting for you."

Thank You, Lord, for the assurance that in heaven we will again be with our loved ones and have bodies like Your very own. Amen.

The Triumph Was Ours

Jennifer Lis

For I am persuaded that neither death nor life, nor angels nor princi-palities nor powers, nor things present nor things to come, nor height nor depth, nor any other created thing, shall be able to separate us from the love of God which is in Christ Jesus our Lord. (Romans 8:38-39, NKJV)

It was just him and me alone in the quiet room. The hospital staff had retreated out of respect for our need for privacy. There were no family, no sound of screaming ambulances, no ventilators or IV bags of chemotherapy. After a year and a half, the cancer that had invaded Rick's body and our lives was bringing our time to-gether to a close.

His level of consciousness drifted, and I sensed I didn't have much time. First I prayed for him, stroking the dear, bald head that had suffered through so much. As I touched him, I remem-bered him as he was from the first day we'd met, always consis-tent in his affection and gentleness. His total acceptance of me, his forgiveness, his refusal to hear anything negative about me, painted a radiant picture of the heavenly Father's love.

I loved my husband deeply and now began to prepare my heart to give him my best.

I sang to him. I sang not only to keep the darkness away but also to shine the Father's love onto his face. "Because the Lord is my shepherd, I have everything that I need."

Slowly the dull, glassy eyes focused once again.

"Even when walking through the dark valley of death . . . I will never be afraid, for He is there beside me."

As the song reached its triumphant end, my heart swelled with tenderness for Rick and for the Lord he would soon see.

He couldn't speak, couldn't even move his mouth, but his eyes were full of such an overwhelming love I could hardly look into them. It was a reflection from the throne of God Himself. A beautiful sunburst from behind the clouds—and then he was gone.

Death had come and reclaimed his body, but the triumph was ours, thanks to our victorious Savior. Love once more proved to be as strong as death. I knew my pain was coming and it would take a long time to dull, but at that moment I knew God had accepted my most precious gift—the dear husband He had lent to me.

Lord, I thank You for showing me how strong love is when the bond is founded on You. Thank You for the knowledge and deep soul-assurance that love is every bit as strong as death. My glory is in Your victory over sin and the grave. May I be a humble witness to the power of a marriage blessed and guided by You, even when You lead to the gates of death itself, for now I see that is only the beginning of reality. Amen.

Marriage is . . .

the sunrise and the sunset
those times when night melds
with morning
and day becomes evening
a blending of those qualities that
are altogether different
and yet absolutely the same.

— *J.L. Hardesty*

Wedding Vows
Marie DisBrow

When I stood beside you at the altar,
repeating solemn vows before the Lord,
I was completely unaware
of the challenges
    the joys
    the sorrows
that the future held in store.

All I could see was love and dreams,
red roses climbing up a picket fence,
perfect children with eyes of blue,
romantic moments
    a house
    good success
never-ending happiness.

Looking back over years gone by,
I now can clearly see
How hardships made us stronger,
brought us ever closer
    to each other
    to our God
and to eternity.

Meet the Authors

Candace F. (Candy) Abbott is the founder of Delmarva Christian Writers' Fellowship. She is the author of *Fruit-Bearer: What Can I Do for You, Lord?* Candy and her husband, Drew, are owners of Fruit-Bearer Publishing. She may be reached at P.O. Box 777, Georgetown, DE 19947; phone: 302-856-6649; fax: 302-856-7742; e-mail: dabbott@dmv.com.

Charlotte Adelsperger is the author of several books and has written for more than seventy-five publications and compilations. She coauthored with her daughter, Karen Hayse, a small gift book, *Through the Generations: The Unique Call of Motherhood.* Her credits include *Woman's World,* Focus on the Family's *LifeWise* and *Clubhouse* and *Stories for a Woman's Heart: The Second Collection,* compiled by Alice Gray. Charlotte enjoys speaking to women's groups and may be contacted at author04@aol.com.

Candy Arrington's publishing credits include *The Upper Room, Discipleship Journal, Christian Home & School* and family.org (Focus on the Family). She is a contributor to *What's in the Bible for*™ . . . *Couples* (Starburst Publishers) and is currently under contract to coauthor a recovery book for suicide survivors scheduled for publication in 2003. Candy and her husband, Jim, have been married for twenty-two years, have two children and live in Spartanburg, South Carolina, where Candy is a choir member, youth discipleship leader and frequent contributor to the monthly church magazine. (CNAnSptbg@aol.com)

BaBette Z. Bechtold lives in the Pacific Northwest with her husband of fourteen years and their three daughters, whom she homeschools. She has been writing professionally for the past five years. After graduating from Northwest College in 1983, BaBette worked for ten years as a chaplain/counselor at the King County Department of Youth Services with at-risk youth. She has also served in children's ministries. Currently she codirects the women's ministry at her church. In her spare time she enjoys sewing, crafts and reading.

Earlene D. Benson is a wife and a mother, a teacher and a freelance writer. With her farmer-husband of over fifty years, she is now serving the Lord in Puerto Rico. They have served for seven years at Safe Harbor, the mission for the Roosevelt Roads Naval Base. For the past four years they have been at the Evangelical School for the Deaf. "Wearing all those hats, I have never run out of topics to write about," she says. They have four children, eight grandchildren and one great-granddaughter.

Sharon Bridgewater at age forty-five acted on a desire to write that had lingered since high school. Since then she has written four novels: a murder mystery, a WWII war story, a Civil War western and a romance. A musician by talent and a bookkeeper by trade, Sharon's belief in God and her own moral ethics compel her to write wholesome material. She hopes to cause her readers to think about spiritual ideals or, at the very least, to entertainingly lighten their everyday loads.

Debbie Brockett is a freelance writer who lives in Colorado. She wrote a monthly column for a regional Christian magazine, *The Testimony*, for six years and cofounded Western Slope Christian Writers' Association. She has contributed stories to three books. Her first historical fiction novel, *Stained Glass Rose*, was released in 2002.

Brandy S. Brow admits that she and her husband were not madly in love when they married on Valentine's Day in 1993. "It is by God's grace that Jim and I made it through those difficult years learning to love each other and learning how to continually keep our vows. As our faith and marriage have grown, so has our family. When I'm not caring for our four children, homeschooling or being with my husband, I write children's stories, devotionals and articles for women, parents and families."

Georgia E. Burkett has been writing newspaper articles, devotionals for several publications and short inspirational stories for magazines and historical publications since she was in high school. Now eighty-one years old, Georgia devotes most of her time to her church, family and wide circle of friends. She also sings with a group of seniors, The Happy Wanderers, for nursing homes, senior centers and other local functions.

Dianne E. Butts' work has appeared over 125 times in 50 publications, including *Focus on the Family* magazine. She recently published her first book, *Dear America: A Letter of Comfort and Hope to a Grieving Nation* (Ampelos Press, 2002). Dianne says, "When crisis hits, we all ask 'Why?' and 'Is God there?' *Dear America* offers some answers I found through my own crises and grief." When she's not writing, Dianne enjoys riding motorcycles with her husband, Hal. Dianne can be contacted at P.O. Box 901, Limon, CO 80828. Learn more about *Dear America* at her Web site: www.DianneEButts.com.

Sue Cameron loves being, among other things, a Bible teacher, speaker and writer. But most of all she loves the fact that she and her husband, Craig, have enjoyed twenty-five years of sharing their hearts, souls and lives. Just when she felt she couldn't hold one more ounce of God's blessing, she became "Grammy Sue." Then two son-in-laws were added to their family! "Truly goodness and mercy are following me!" Sue says. "I am most grateful."

Jana Carman and her husband, John, a retired pastor, have four children and seven grandchildren. She is past president and longtime board member of the St. Davids Christian Writers' Association. Jana is the coauthor of *People Like Us* and author of *People of Faith*, both published by Lillenas Drama. A piano teacher for many years, Jana has also served as choir director, soloist, organist and pianist. "Music, drama and writing are intertwined in my life—'a triple-braided cord . . . not easily broken' " (Ecclesiastes 4:12, TLB).

Carol Carolan and her husband, John, have been married for twenty-seven years. She is the mother of two grown children. Carol came to know the Lord thirteen years ago. That's when she started sharing God's stories. As a storyteller, she worked for Miss Margie's Pee Wee Gym. Carol and Miss Margie became friends and are now partners in a Christian childcare center where Christ is the center of the program. Carol also started writing her stories and says, "God certainly stretches us when we give our lives to Him!"

Martha Marlow Carpenter is a fifty-three-year-old mother and grandmother. She teaches an adult Sunday school class, works with the youth ministry and writes a column for her local paper. Martha also teaches a women's Bible study and feels privileged to counsel and mentor young women. Although her husband's breathing difficulties have worsened, he is still mobile and enjoys getting out every day. Along with fatigue and muscle pain, he suffers from multiple chemical sensitivity and must be careful when going anywhere in public. "Our life is different now; perhaps difficult, but sweeter," Martha says.

Daniel Christian is the pen name for a man who had the courage to confess and, with God's help, overcome a sexual addiction that could have destroyed his marriage and his family. Today Daniel and Ariane continue to draw closer to one another and to the Lord. Communication, a lot of laughs and giggles together, as well as praying with and for one another are included in the reconstruction materials that now shape their marriage to be built into something stronger than ever in Christ.

Brenda R. Coats and her husband, Shaun, reside in northern Colorado and recently celebrated their twelfth anniversary. In addition to writing, Brenda enjoys playing the piano, reading and watching professional football every Sunday with her family. Shaun is a senior prototype machinist and is preparing for full-time pastoral ministry. They have three homeschooled children—Ashlee, Jessica and Andrew.

Leslie Trent Conger is a writer and teacher whose passion is developing intimacy with God through praying the Psalms. She wrote a curriculum for a year's study of the Psalms for a women's Bible study within her church and cotaught a series of classes with an associate pastor entitled "Learning to Pray the Psalms." She has also written for an annual Advent devotional book sponsored by her congregation, First Presbyterian Church. Leslie now serves as editor for this project. Currently she is working on a novel for children. Leslie lives in Boulder, Colorado, with her husband.

Marty Cottrill was born in Columbus, Ohio, and now lives near Dayton, Ohio. She and her husband married in 1962 and now have two grown children, two granddaughters and one grandson. The Cottrills have made twelve long-distance moves during their marriage. Along the way, Marty has written devotionals, radio spots, articles for denominational publications and reflective prose and verse. She especially enjoys writing memoir and biographical sketches of ancestors and journaling for and about her grandchildren. Marty works for a curriculum development corporation.

Marie DisBrow was raised in San Antonio, Texas. From a young age, her great-aunt kept her supplied with books and introduced her to the joys of the public library. Her love of writing arose from her lifelong love of reading. Marie resides with her husband in a wooded area of northern California. After years of living in a big city and working as an electronics technician, she now enjoys a much simpler life. She writes poetry, devotionals and articles and has a semi-autobiographical novel in progress.

Bonnie Doran is a part-time bookkeeper and freelance writer in Littleton, Colorado. She has been married for nineteen years and has three cats. Her writing credits include articles for *The Lutheran Journal, My Turn to Care, Pathways to God, The Secret Place, The Upper Room* and *Woman's Touch*. Bonnie was a short-term missionary for two years with the Far East Broadcasting Company in Okinawa, Japan, where she served as secretary, scriptwriter and programmer. She enjoys writing, cooking, playing the flute and scuba diving.

Steve Dunham and Elise have been married since 1974. They have six children and live in Virginia. Steve has been a writer and editor for more than twenty years and writes two newspaper columns, "Commuter Crossroads" and "Off the Deep End." His e-mail address is Literalman@aol.com. His Web site is www.stevedunham.50megs.com.

Jim Dyet and his wife, Gloria, reside in Colorado Springs, where Jim works from home as product development manager for The Amy Foundation. He also serves Cook Communications as a part-time theological consultant and preaches in area churches. His most recent books are *No-Brainer's Guide to the Bible* and *Overcoming Subtle Sins*. Jim and Gloria have three adult children.

June Eaton is a retired classroom teacher now actively involved in a freelance writing/teaching ministry. In addition to writing hundreds of articles and stories, she has cowritten seven Christian books for an international publisher. She and her husband, Fred, have been married for forty-six years. They are the parents of three lovely daughters and proud grandparents of five. Their home is near Chicago.

Eva Marie Everson and her husband, Dennis, have been married for over twenty-three years. They have four children and three precious grandchildren. Eva Marie writes fiction and nonfiction. Her works include two books on marriage, *True Love* and *One True Vow,* both published by Barbour/Promise Press and released in 2000 and 2001 respectively.

Milton Fisher is professor emeritus of Old Testament, Reformed Episcopal Seminary, Philadelphia. *Merilyn* keeps her nurse's registration active to serve as volunteer camp nurse each summer. They now reside at Quarryville Presbyterian Retirement Community in Lancaster County, Pennsylvania, where both have opportunity to employ their respective training and experience. Milton is a member of Northeast Presbytery of the Associate Reformed Presbyterian Church.

Anita L. Fordyce is the public relations manager at Grand View Hospital in Sellersville, Pennsylvania. She has been a professional writer since the late '70s, writing newspaper features, columns and Christian magazine and devotional articles. Most recently she has published a newspaper series about grandparenting entitled "What Sound Does a Giraffe Make?" Married for thirty-five years, Anita and her husband, a minister of Christian education, have two grown daughters and six grandsons.

Sharon Gibson was raised in Zaire, Africa, by missionary parents. She has served three terms in the Kansas legislature as a state representative, owned two inspirational gift stores and been a product manager for Day-Spring Cards. At present, she writes and stays home to care for the children she and her husband adopted.

Amy Givler met her husband when they were both in medical school. They work at an indigent-care hospital (she part-time, he full-time) and are raising three children in Monroe, Louisiana. She writes *HomeLife* magazine's health column and is the author of *Hope in the Face of Cancer* (Harvest House Publishers, 2003), a book for people who have recently been diagnosed with cancer.

Verda J. Glick, a missionary in El Salvador for thirty-six years, praises God for protection during war, her husband's kidnapping and numerous armed robberies. Her book, *Deliver the Ransom Alone,* tells how her son met with the kidnappers and pleaded for his father's release. She can be contacted at verda@tutopia.com.

Patricia R. Gottschalk has been married for forty-five years. She has three married children and six grandchildren. After working part-time in several clerical positions, Pat has retired but continues to volunteer two days a week with a Christian nonprofit agency which helps people who are going through employment transition. She is on the Mission Group of her church and spends time being a stateside contact person for a number of young missionary friends.

Marilynn Griffith is a freelance writer living in Florida with her husband and six homeschooled children. Her recent publishing credits include *Honey for a Homeschooler's Heart, Crumbs in the Keyboard*, *Christian Families Online* and more. Marilynn and her family are active in their local church where her husband is a deacon. They have been married for ten years.

Marcia A. Gruver and her husband, Lee, have one daughter and four sons. "Collectively," Marcia says, "this motley crew has graced us with seven grandchildren." Lee is an oil and gas landman. Marcia is the Children's Church director for the three- to five-year-olds at Victory Christian Center in Kingwood, Texas, where she has written curriculum and skits for the children's department.

Nancy Hagerman is a writer and popular speaker in western Colorado. She accepted Jesus as her Savior while in high school and graduated from Intermountain Bible College. Her husband, Steven, is founder and director of Turkish World Outreach, a ministry to Turks worldwide. The couple have a grown son and daughter. Two granddaughters and an infant grandson keep them busy. Nancy is the author of *In the Pit: A Testimony of God's Faithfulness to a Bipolar Christian*. Visit her Web site at http://users.acsol.net/~hagerman.

Pam Halter and her husband, Daryl, have been married for eleven and a half years. They have two daughters, Anna (who is autistic) and Mary. Daryl is a music teacher. Pam is a homeschooling mom and children's book author. Concordia Publishing House has released her first two books, *Beatrice Loses Her Doll* and *Beatrice's New Clothes*.

J.L. (Jo) Hardesty is the author of *The Lost Legend of the First Christmas* and *Escape to Egypt*—Books One and Two of The Lost Legend Trilogy. A writer and graphic designer for more than thirty years, Jo has been the editor of four national magazines. Additionally she has contributed literally hundreds of articles to numerous major national and international periodicals. Jo has been happily married for just under fourteen years to a man fifteen years her junior. The mother of two sons and a daughter, Jo has seven grandchildren. Today she is focusing on her career as a novelist, specializing in Christian and crossover fiction.

Jeannie Harmon has been married to Pat for twenty-nine years. Pat is a HVAC specialist for a computer storage company, and Jeannie is a freelance writer. She has written more than twenty children's books and an adult e-book, *Become a Children's Book Author,* published by www.Fabjob.com. They have two children and two grandchildren.

Lydia Harris is a freelance writer from Seattle. Her articles, devotions, book reviews and stories have appeared in numerous publications, including *Stories for the Heart* and Focus on the Family's *LifeWise* magazine. Her column, "A Cup of Tea with Lydia," is published across the United States and Canada. In 2000 she received the Oregon Christian Writer of the Year award. A former schoolteacher, she teaches at writers' conferences. Lydia and her husband of thirty-five years, Milt, have two married children and two adorable grandsons.

Paula Harris is the director of Transformed Women's Ministries (Romans 12:1-2). She resides in Exton, Pennsylvania, with her wonderful husband, William. They have three sons: Andre, Aaron and Arlen. Paula is an inspirational speaker and teacher who delights in equipping others in their search for truth from the Word of God. You may visit her Web site at www.twmforjesus.org.

Kathleen Hayes is the senior editor of *The Secret Place*, a daily devotional guide published by the American Baptist Churches in the USA, as well as an editor for the Philadelphia Mennonite High School and Christian Community Health Fellowship. She is also the author of *Women on the*

Threshold: Voices of Salvadoran Baptist Women. Kathleen and Jeff, a Presbyterian minister, were married in 1997. They have no children but provide lots of TLC for two dogs and two cats.

Brenda Hendricks received Jesus as her personal Savior when she was nine. She has taught Sunday school since she was seventeen, a Good News Club for two years and a high school Released Time class for three years. She has been married for over twenty-seven years. She and her husband have two daughters and one grandson. Brenda owns and operates her own dog-grooming business.

Barbara Hibschman team-teaches at marriage retreats with her husband, Jim. She is a pastor's wife, mother, grandmother, former missionary to the Philippines and teacher. Barbara is a popular speaker for women's ministries and missions and Christian education conferences. She has written hundreds of magazine articles and is the author of eight books and a contributing author to nine devotional books.

Bob Hostetler (http://www.bobhostetler.com) is an award-winning author, editor, pastor and speaker from southwestern Ohio. His thirteen books, which include *They Call Me A.W.O.L.* and *Holy Moses (and Other Adventures in Vertical Living)*, have sold over 2 million copies. He has coauthored many books with Josh McDowell. Bob and his wife, Robin, are among the leaders of Cobblestone Community Church in Oxford, Ohio. They have a daughter, Aubrey, and a son, Aaron. Bob and Robin have been foster parents to ten boys—though not all at once!

Betsy Howard is the pen name of an occupational therapist who works with learning-disabled students. Since her days as a young Christian mother, she has been a prayer warrior for children. Standing in faith through their daughter's thirteen-year battle with schizophrenia, she and her husband, Will, look to the Lord daily for strength—and wait for a miracle.

Judith Howard and her husband, Frank, were married for thirty-nine years and enjoyed their blended family of two boys and a girl. Frank, a realtor, encouraged Judy, a former church professional, to write more articles and to keep trying to get those novels published. He's now cheering her on from heaven.

Michele T. Huey (www.geocities.com/michelehuey) writes two weekly newspaper columns and writes and records a daily two-minute devotional for a local radio station. A collection of her meditations, *Minute Meditations: Meeting God in Everyday Experiences*, was published by Ampelos Press in April 2000. Her work has appeared in *Guideposts, The Upper Room* and *Chicken Soup for the Christian Family Soul*. An English teacher at a local Christian school, Michele is a member of the St. Davids Christian Writers' Association board of directors and also teaches workshops on writing.

Joy R. Jacobs' greatest joys are spending time with her Father in the Word, working with the women of her church, writing and enjoying her family—especially her five grandchildren. Joy and Bob met at Messiah College in 1963, a year after the formation of the Jacobs Brothers Evangelistic Association. In 1977 the Jacobs Brothers founded the King's Kids' Camp to minister to underprivileged children. Joy works for Shepherd's Touch Counseling Ministries and serves as director of counseling at Daybreak Christian and Missionary Alliance Church, Mechanicsburg, Pennsylvania. She has authored several devotional books.

Diana L. James (www.DianaJames.com) is the author/editor/compiler of the Bounce Back book series (Christian Publications, Inc.) that include *Bounce Back, You Can Bounce Back Too, Teens Can Bounce Back* and *Families Can Bounce Back*. Diana's stories and articles have also appeared in numerous magazines and book compilations. She is a group leader with CLASS (Christian Leaders, Authors and Speakers Seminars) and a former board member of National Speakers Association, Los Angeles Chapter. Diana speaks for churches, writers' conferences, retreats and Christian women's groups.

Dawn Janho has been married to Tim for fourteen years. At age sixteen they became high school sweethearts and married at age nineteen. They have two wonderful children, TJ (ten) and Nicole (nine). Dawn is an active leader in the women's ministries at her church. She has led several Bible studies, shared her testimony and been a speaker for various MOPS groups on Time Management and Organizational Skills. You may contact her at Djanho@aol.com.

Betty J. Johnson and her husband live in Parker, Colorado, where she is involved in family activities, continues as a freelance writer and frequently speaks at MOPS meetings. Her articles and devotions have appeared in numerous magazines and books including *Stories for a Woman's Heart* (Multnomah Publishers), *Season's of a Woman's Heart* (Starburst Publishers) and *Teatime Stories for Mothers* (RiverOak Publishing).

Clint Kelly is a humorist, four-time dad and writer of fiction. He and his bride, Cheryll, have been married for thirty years despite the writing/publishing of five adventure novels and three parenting books. Clint's latest books are *Dare to Raise Exceptional Children* (Albury Publishing) and *Escape Underground* (Focus on the Family/Bethany House Publishers).

Virelle Kidder is the host of *Real Life*, a daily radio show in the capital district of New York. She is the author of three books: *Mothering Upstream; Loving, Launching and Letting Go,* and *Getting the Best Out of Public Schools* (coauthored with her husband, Steve). She is also a contributing writer to *Today's Christian Woman*. Virelle loves to encourage women on their spiritual journeys.

Gail Black Kopf, a Canadian freelance writer, is the author of *Rubicon* (Thomas Nelson, 1993) and has won awards from the Greater Philadelphia Christian Writers' Conference, *Campus Life*, *Writer's Digest* and Gardenia Press. With numerous magazine and newspaper articles published, she is currently working on her third novel. She resides in Summersville, West Virginia.

Tina Krause is a wife, mother and "Nana" to grandsons Ian and Isaac. She and her husband, Jim, live in Valparaiso, Indiana, where they enjoy empty-nest living. As an award-winning newspaper columnist and freelance writer, Tina has authored over 750 published articles in the past twelve years. She is the author of *Laughter Therapy* (Barbour Publishers/Promise Press) and has contributed to eight devotional books. Tina is a frequent speaker at women's retreats, workshops and church banquets.

Miggy Krentel, grandmother of eleven and boasting of one great-grandchild, lives in a retirement community in Rexford, New York. She has authored two nonfiction books and two children's books and contributes to various Christian magazines. Writing is her passion and

Scrabble is her delight. Her latest book is *Straight from a Widow's Heart* (Cook Communications Ministries).

Lenné Kugler-Hunt was trained as a clinical psychologist and has spent the past seventeen years tending the wounds of others. In addition, she has spent the past decade as a full-time professor of psychology. In May 2001 God called her away from all of that and directed her to begin an art business, Deep Unto Deep Designs, which produces stationery and artwork centered around the name, Word and glory of God. She can be contacted at deep_unto_deep.nc@att.net. At a TACF Healing Conference in November 2001, the Lord completely healed Kris, her husband, after six years of illness.

Faye Landrum is a retired registered nurse and has been a freelance writer since 1967. Her work has been published in more than 220 Christian and secular publications. She is also the coauthor of two books for children, *Midweek Messages* and *86 Crafts from Plastic Castoffs*. In 1999 Tyndale House Publishers released her latest book, *The Final Mile: A Wife's Response to Her Husband's Terminal Illness*. You can reach Faye at FAYELAND@aol.com.

Carmen Leal is the author of *Faces of Huntington's* and *Portraits of Huntington's*. These days, when she's not visiting David in the nursing home, she speaks internationally on Huntington's and caregiving topics.

Linda S. Lee (Mamalee50@home.com) is a Bible study leader, speaker and coleader of a home group through her church. Now living in Indiana with her husband, this California freelancer has lived from the Pacific Islands to the British Isles. Linda writes for various publications and recently served as a columnist for Comcast's www.InYourTown.com. Her hobbies include sailing, reading and sewing. Her heart is for strong marriages and families. Linda and her husband, Terry, speak in churches to encourage couples that marriage can overcome even adultery if both parties submit to the lordship of Christ.

Elsie Lippy and her husband, Bruce, have served for many years with Child Evangelism Fellowship in Warrenton, Missouri. Bruce enjoys helping missionaries develop video presentations. Elsie is editor of

Evangelizing Today's Child magazine, a publication that helps church and club teachers evangelize and disciple young children.

Jennifer Lis has been widowed for two and a half years after a twenty-six-year marriage. She is employed at the local hospital and writes not only on the side, "but all the way around." Her hobbies include spinning, knitting and gardening. Jennifer attends a Baptist church and enjoys singing in the choir.

Marita Littauer is a professional speaker with over twenty-five years' experience. She is the author of ten books, including *Personality Puzzle, Talking So People Will Listen* and *Love Extravagantly*. Marita is the president of CLASServices Inc., an organization that provides resources, training and promotion for speakers and authors. Marita and her husband, Chuck Noon, have been married since 1983. For more information on Marita and/or CLASS, please visit www.classervices.com or call 800-433-6633.

Susan A.J. Lyttek, wife of Gary since 1983 and homeschool mother of two boys, has published stories, articles, curriculum, interviews, a column, plays, poems, devotions and cards. She's also authored six books of dramatic monologues. Susan has several books under publishing consideration, including *Dinosaur Window*, her Christian adventure/fantasy series for boys eight to twelve.

Therese "Terry" Martin spent her formative years in many of the geographic hot spots of the 1950s and 1960s—Vietnam, Laos and Liberia. After her father's retirement from the Foreign Service, the family settled in California just in time for the social upheavals of the late '60s. "This 'calm, tranquil, uneventful' upbringing may have helped prepare me to survive raising four sons and homeschooling three of them," Terry says. She presently lives in Colorado with her husband and two youngest sons and is involved in education and foreign missions.

Jean R. Mays, a newcomer to Christian writing and publishing, is focusing her long-time writing/editing skills (she is editor of her Colorado mountain community newspaper, *The Big Elk Bugle*), on God-impacted personal experiences and biblical insights. Jean's husband, now deceased, Lt. Col. Raymond R. Mays, U.S. Navy, was a topographical engineer. Born and married into the military (and raised around the world), Jean also served. She was a Lt. JG, U.S. Naval Reserve, as a WAVE, in World War II.

Lucinda Secrest McDowell, a graduate of Gordon-Conwell Theological Seminary, is a national conference speaker and author of four books: *Quilts From Heaven, Women's Spiritual Passages, Amazed by Grace* and *A Southern-Style Christmas*. She lives in New England with her husband of eighteen years and her four children. Visit her Web site: http://www.EncouragingWords.net.

Wanda McGlinchey-Ryan, a freelance writer since her retirement from a career as a chemist, lives in Chester County, Pennsylvania. Her first published article, "Called Home from the Course," told the tale of her second husband's death of a heart attack on a golf course and the reasons his golf buddies hope to die there too. That publication led to writing assignments that afford her the opportunity to interview and write about a wide variety of fascinating people.

Kathleen Swartz McQuaig, after twenty plus years of marriage and simultaneously raising teenagers and a toddler, writes and speaks about what is closest to her heart—marriage and family. Her poems, devotionals and personal-experience stories stem from a desire to encourage others with our Lord's gentle reminders that touch everyday life. She facilitates a public speaking course for military officers at the Army War College in Carlisle, Pennsylvania.

Edward E. Menaldino has been married for fifty-four years and is the father of three children and grandfather of six. He pastored in San Francisco, Minneapolis and Philadelphia. Ed has been a family camp speaker in all the major camps for the Pentecostal Assemblies of Canada, as well as a youth camp speaker in the United States, Canada and Poland and at youth conventions in Italy. Presently he serves as guest teacher and lecturer at the Warsaw Theological Seminary.

Ginnie Mesibov is a freelance writer and the parish support coordinator for Tenth Presbyterian Church, Philadelphia. Her inspirational column, "Woman's Corner," appears each month in the *Woodland Newsletter* published by Woodland Presbyterian Church, Philadelphia.

Ginnie is a popular Bible study leader. She attended Philadelphia Biblical University and graduated from Clarke Conservatory of Music with a diploma in piano pedagogy. Ginnie and her husband, Harold, have been married for thirty years.

Kathy Collard Miller and her husband, Larry, have been married for thirty-one years. Together they are the authors of forty-five books, including *What's in the Bible for* ™ . . . *Couples* and *When the Honeymoon's Over.* They have spoken across the United States and internationally and are both members of the National Speakers Association (NSA). Kathy's latest book is *The Un-Devotional for Teens: Fun Puzzles to Help You Learn Scripture.*

Diane Mitchell and her husband, Les, have been married for thirty-eight years. They now reside in Oneida, New York, near their children and grandchildren. Diane is the executive director of Heritage Farms, Inc., a ministry to individuals with developmental disabilities. Diane says she and Les are an example of opposites attracting. Les is an introvert; Diane an extrovert. Les is very athletic and outdoorsy; Diane would rather sit cuddled up with a good book. Les is a realist; Diane a diehard romantic. Together they've learned it takes both the soil and the fertilizer to bring forth the rose.

Jane Moran has been happily married for nine years. Originally from Pennsylvania, she and her husband, Tony, live in Hope Mills, North Carolina, with their daughters, Laurel and Clara. A librarian by profession, Jane considers her most significant job title to be "Mommy." Tony and Jane are active in small group leadership at their church. Jane is also active in her local Christian writer's group, community theater and a fledgling church drama ministry.

Lynn D. Morrissey is founder of the ministry Noteworthy Living, editor of the best-selling devotionals *Seasons of a Woman's Heart* and *Treasures of a Woman's Heart,* contributing author to numerous best-selling devotional books; and CLASSpeaker and staff member who specializes in prayer-journaling and women's topics.

Cecil ("Cec") Murphey has written, cowritten or ghostwritten ninety books, including *Seeking God's Hidden Face: When God Seems Absent* (InterVarsity Press), *The God Who Pursues: Encountering a Relentless God*

(Bethany House Publishers) and *Futuring: Leading Your Church into Tomorrow,* cowritten with Dr. Samuel Chand (Baker Books). He has ghostwritten autobiographies for well-known personalities including Franklin Graham, singer B.J. Thomas, pianist Dino Karsanakas and the million-copies-sold *Gifted Hands: The Ben Carson Story*.

Jill Nelson and her husband, Doug, recently celebrated their twentieth anniversary. They reside in rural Minnesota with their four children and a jail-breaking hamster that likes to chew carpet. Jill holds a B.A. in literature and creative writing and employs her talents authoring public relations material for the health care facility where she works. She is actively seeking publication of her first novel.

Brenda Nixon and her husband, Paul, have been married for twenty-three years and are the parents of two adventurous daughters. Brenda is a professional speaker on parenting the young child, contributing author to five books and the author of *Parenting Power in the Early Years*. She may be contacted on-line at www.parentpwr.com or by calling 740-397-8466.

Chuck Noon (chucknoon.com) is a professional counselor licensed in two states. He has worked with hundreds of families and couples in many varieties of settings. Chuck offers marriage tele-coaching, two-day intensive marriage therapy, spouse candidate assessment, singles programs and marriage workshops and seminars that can be presented jointly with Marita. Their book on making the modern marriage work, *Love Extravagantly*, was released in July 2001, and they are working on *Kick the Tires Before You Buy: Your Guide to Spouse Candidate Assessment*. Chuck enjoys mountain biking and motorcycling. He and Marita rollerblade, sail and scuba dive. Together they collect vintage vehicles.

Gwen Northcutt is an eighty-year-old widow who lives in a retirement community in Solomons, Maryland. She is legally blind and leads her community's Low Vision Group. Her two married children live in Maryland. Gwen has always been a writer and has edited three newsletters. Other creative pursuits have included sewing, needlework, crafts, cooking and growing plants—including orchids.

Karen O'Connor is an award-winning author, Bible teacher and popular speaker at retreats and other events. She was chosen Writer of the

Year by the San Diego Christian Writers' Guild in 1997. The same organization named her book, *Basket of Blessings: 31 Days to a More Grateful Heart,* the Best Book Published in 1998. She lives in San Diego with her husband, Charles Flowers. The couple has five children and eleven grandchildren. Contact Karen at www.karenoconnor.com

Jean M. Olsen and her husband spent thirty-two of their fifty years together in Africa developing gifts they didn't know they possessed and which they still enjoy using. For Jean this included piano teaching and secretarial work. She began writing "A.A." (after Africa). The Olsens live in New Jersey and have two married daughters and four grandchildren.

Janet Packard welcomes your comments and questions regarding couples praying together. Approaching the "empty nest" in 1986, she returned to Mesa State College and discovered a new passion: the craft of writing. She researches and writes family history and has published articles in *The Secret Place, We Remember the Fabulous '50s* and *The Testimony.* In 2002 Janet established Janella Press to publish her children's storybook, *The Quail's Quest.* The importance of parental protection is the theme of this beautifully illustrated book. Phone toll free 1-877-301-5669 or e-mail Milt_JanPackard@msn.com.

Kate Paffett is a freelance writer from Drexel Hill, Pennsylvania. Her articles have appeared in magazines such as *Liguorian, Catholic Digest* and *Celebrate Life.* She is also a contributing author to *My Turn to Care: Encouragement for Caregivers of Aging Parents.* Many of Kate's articles are written about people she has met while volunteering in her parish community. From bringing communion to the homebound to chaperoning 150 teenagers on a bus trip from Philly to Denver to celebrate World Youth Day, Kate has many stories to tell! She and her husband, Bill, celebrated their twenty-fifth wedding anniversary in 2002 and have three children.

Jean Pence is a child of God, wife, homeschool mother of one and youth leader, currently living in Delaware. She enjoys learning about life from her six-year-old daughter, encouraging her husband in his ministry, reading, walking on the beach and quilting. Jean has always had a passion for putting words on a page but has only recently begun to share these words with others. She commits all of her writing to the Lord. It is her prayer that you are blessed by what you read.

Tracie Peterson is a best-selling, award-winning author of over forty-five fiction titles and one nonfiction baby gift book. She lives and writes in Belgrade, Montana. As a Christian, wife, mother, writer, editor and speaker (in that order), Tracie finds her slate quite full. "I find myself blessed to be able to work at a job I love," Tracie says. "I get to travel, study history, spin yarns, spend time with my family and hopefully glorify God. I can't imagine a more perfect arrangement."

Susan Petropulos is a wife of thirty years, mother of two and soon-to-be grandma. For the past seven years she has been in ministry at North Way Christian Community; she is presently serving as a ministry associate in the area of spiritual growth, which includes writing curriculum and spiritual growth materials. Sue coauthored two companion devotional journals with Pastor Dave Fleming titled *Drawn by the Light* and *Turning Points: Reflections on the Journey of Repentance through the Season of Lent.* She has been a freelance writer for fifteen years and has been published in devotional magazines.

Vickie Phelps is the author of *101 Keys For Life* and *May Christ Be the Center of Your Christmas,* both published by Barbour Publishing. She is the coauthor of an electronic book, *How to Write for the Christian Marketplace* (Deep South Publishing, http://www.writersweekly.com/shop/specializedmarkets.html#6). Vickie is also a contributor to *Seasons of a Woman's Heart* and *God's Little Rule Book* (Starburst Publishers), *The Writers' Journal Guide to the Writing Life* (Writers' Journal Books) and *The Best of The Proverbs 31 Ministry* (Proverbs 31 Ministry).

Steffani Powell, MSN, lives on a ranch in central Texas with her family. A Christian counselor on a part-time basis, her priority has been homeschooling their children and farming their land. Now that the children are getting older, Steffani hopes to indulge her lifelong love of writing. Topics she addresses include marriage and family, spiritual abuse in the church and sexual abuse and addiction. Seeking to apply biblical principles and the love of Christ to those who are hurting emotionally, both through writing and counseling, is her passion.

Myrna Pugh lives in Lakewood, Colorado, and Tucson, Arizona, with her husband, Pat, who is a physician. She holds a master's degree in counseling from Denver Seminary. Myrna writes and speaks about issues that impact women in the Church, such as single parenting, abuse and recovery issues and how suffering conforms us to the image of Christ. She was a single parent of five after she was widowed. She was a "late bloomer" who took twenty-seven years to finish college, not including graduate school. Myrna is also a Stephen Series trainer.

Lee Roddy is a best-selling author. He has written fifty published novels and fifteen nonfiction books with sales in the millions of copies. His credits include *Grizzly Adams*, which became a prime-time television series; *The Lincoln Conspiracy*, which made the *New York Times* best-seller list; *Jesus*, now a film in more than 500 languages; and four series of character-development novels for young adults and readers ages eight to twelve. Visit his Web site at www.leeroddybooks.com. Lee and Cicely have been married for fifty-five years.

Jim Russell is the founder of the Amy Writing Awards, acclaimed as the nation's most popular journalism competition. The contest's annual cash prizes inspire writers to "decisively quote the Word of God" in articles printed in secular publications. (www.amyfound.org)

Wanda G. Schwandt and her husband, Mark, live in Pennsylvania with their two wonderful teenagers. Wanda writes devotions, inspirational articles and short stories. She also manages the content for www.wandawrites.com and www.intimateprayer.com. Her family enjoys traveling, camping and scouting together.

Alexandra Scott (pen name) and her husband, Jonathan, have been married for twelve years. They have two sons, Elijah and David. Jonathan is a lawyer. Alexandra is a freelance writer, editor and author. They live in Los Angeles, California.

Laney Scott (pen name) has been married for over twenty years and is still learning to love and forgive the way Jesus does. She lives in Virginia within sight of the Blue Ridge Mountains with her husband and children. A writer and teacher, she enjoys the beauty of flowers, the freshness of dawn and the sight of deer grazing in the fields. More than anything, she longs to know God as deeply and intimately as possible, and she trusts Him to make her feet as "hinds' feet on high places" as she scrambles over the rocky places in life.

Linda Evans Shepherd is a nationally known author and speaker (www.sheppro.com) and the syndicated host of Right to the Heart Radio. She is the founder of Winning Women (www.winningwomen.info), which helps women in women's ministry, as well as AWSA (Advanced Writers and Speakers Association), a support group for Christian women who are both national authors and speakers. Linda lives with her husband and children in Longmont, Colorado.

Mary D. Smith (pen name) is a freelance writer who regularly contributes to several newspapers and children's magazines. She is the mother of two children. Recently she moved to the country, where she enjoys long walks, taking photographs and watching her children grow.

Victoria (Vicki) Smith was raised in the Midwest and met and married her husband, Craig, while attending college. They are now empty-nesters. The Smiths have been in ministry for much of their married life and live in Elizabethtown, Pennsylvania, where Craig is a district executive within the Church of the Brethren. Vicki teaches on spiritual gifts discernment and has a speaking ministry focusing on women's issues of marriage, family and parenting.

Nancy Stoppelkamp (poetnancy@juno.com) wrote poetry as a child and later returned to it as a therapeutic means of coping with a series of overwhelming circumstances, including the death of her mother and sister. She is writing a devotional book called *Singing His Song* to encourage readers to reflect on their own gifts from God and discover the "song" He has written for them. She loves her part-time job at Christian Publications Bookstore. Nancy and her husband, Fred, live on a lake in Ringwood, New Jersey. Fred is a professor at Nyack College. They have three grown children and two precious granddaughters.

Susan Reith Swan and her husband, Tom, live in Pittsburgh, Pennsylvania, with their two children, Nathan and Bethany. She is a librarian, writer, conference coordinator for the Western Pennsylvania chapter of the Society of Children's Book Writers and Illustrators, a former director of the St. Davids Christian Writers' Conference and the freelance editor of *Story Friends* magazine. To relax, Susan enjoys cross-stitching, reading, crafts and nurturing friends and family through her traditional Victorian afternoon teas.

Ann Thorne and her husband of forty-five years have recently moved to the Collegiate Peaks area of Colorado. They both work one day per week in their professions and enjoy the beauty and solitude of the Rockies with hiking and fishing close by. Their lives are busy with prison ministry, serving as mission elders at their church and being part of a strong prayer group within their church and community. Ann reports, "We are truly blessed to be in such beautiful surroundings—a wonderful reminder of God's power and love."

Marjorie Geary Vawter and her husband, Roger, have been married for close to twenty-four years and currently live in Colorado. They have two children, Kathy and Randy. Roger is a project manager for a company that builds churches and other ministry-related buildings. Marjorie teaches English and Spanish at the Christian school where she has been privileged to teach her own children. She is a freelance writer and proofreader and enjoys leading women's Bible studies.

Lynn Ward has been married for twenty-six wonderful years to Steven, with whom she continues to practice the delicate art of compromise. They are the parents of three beautiful, talented daughters who keep her busy shopping, hugging and altering formal gowns.

Linda J. White is a writer living in Virginia. She and her husband, Larry, have been married for thirty-one years and now have their own "zoo" of cats and dogs along with three nearly grown children.

Carolyn Woodie and her husband, Paul, have been married for thirty-seven years and live in Annapolis, Maryland. They have two grown and married children and four grandchildren. After a career as a computer consultant, Carolyn now spends her time enjoying their grandchildren and working as a freelance writer.

Susan Kimmel Wright is the author of the Dead-End Road children's mystery series (Herald Press) as well as many newspaper and magazine articles and devotionals. She is an instructor for the Institute of Children's Literature and a contributing writer to several anthologies, including *God Just Showed Up* (Moody Press). Susan and Dave have been married for over thirty years and are the parents of three teenagers.

Marilyn Yocum and her husband decided to move those 400 miles in 1995 and now reside in Marietta, Ohio, where she is a freelance writer. "Best move we ever made!" she says. "God had all sorts of wonderful people and experiences just waiting here for us!" Her work has appeared in *Moody* magazine, *The Lookout, Discipleship Journal, Guideposts, War Cry, Christian Reader, Devo'Zine, The Upper Room* and other publications.

R.C. Zitzer is a freelance writer living in Alburtis, Pennsylvania, with his wife, Karen; daughter, Holly (now attending Lancaster Bible College); sons Lee, sixteen, and Corey, fourteen; and a psychotic Yorkshire Terrier named Max. "Karen is my love, an artist and homeschool mom," writes R.C. "Holly loves music and being on the go. Lee enjoys breathing life into old muscle cars, and Corey is our graphics expert. When I'm not servicing hospital equipment (my day job), I'm trying to be husband and father and still find time to put pen to paper."

For more information about Marlene Bagnull's ministry, Write His Answer, or to contact her for a speaking engagement, visit her Web site at: www.writehisanswer.com.